The Maya: A Very Short Introduction

VERY SHORT INTRODUCTIONS are for anyone wanting a stimulating and accessible way into a new subject. They are written by experts, and have been translated into more than 45 different languages.

The series began in 1995, and now covers a wide variety of topics in every discipline. The VSI library currently contains over 650 volumes—a Very Short Introduction to everything from Psychology and Philosophy of Science to American History and Relativity—and continues to grow in every subject area.

Very Short Introductions available now:

For more information visit our website

www.oup.com/vsi/

Matthew Restall and Amara Solari

THE MAYA

A Very Short Introduction

OXFORD
UNIVERSITY PRESS

OXFORD

UNIVERSITY PRESS

Oxford University Press is a department of the University of Oxford.
It furthers the University's objective of excellence in research, scholarship,
and education by publishing worldwide. Oxford is a registered trade mark of
Oxford University Press in the UK and certain other countries.

Published in the United States of America by Oxford University Press
198 Madison Avenue, New York, NY 10016, United States of America.

© Oxford University Press 2020

Library of Congress Cataloging-in-Publication Data
2020941766

ISBN 978-0-19-064502-1

1 3 5 7 9 8 6 4 2

Printed in Great Britain by Ashford Colour Press Ltd., Gosport, Hants., on acid-free paper

To the Maya families
who have welcomed us into their homes
and with patience and generosity
have encouraged us to study their past
and helped us to understand their present

Contents

List of illustrations

Chapter 1
Creating "the Maya"

The Maya forged the greatest society in the history of the ancient Americas and one of the great societies in human history. For thousands of years they have lived—and continue to live—in the region that today comprises southern Mexico and its Yucatan Peninsula, Guatemala, Belize, northwestern Honduras, and western El Salvador. Long before contact with Europeans, Maya communities built spectacular cities with large, well-fed populations. They mastered the visual arts and developed a sophisticated writing system that recorded extraordinary knowledge in calendrics, mathematics, and astronomy.

The Maya achieved all this without area-wide centralized control. There was never a single, unified Maya state or empire, but always numerous, evolving ethnic groups speaking distinct Mayan languages. When Europeans invaded the Maya region, it comprised dozens of city-states or kingdoms. Spaniards subsequently carved out colonies in the sixteenth and seventeenth centuries that failed to include or unite the whole region, and in the early twenty-first century it remains divided by modern national boundaries. The Maya have also always been divided geographically because the area's three major regions feature highly contrasting environments—from the flat, arid, riverless limestone peninsula in the north, to the hilly, tropical rainforest of the center, to the volcanic highlands of the south. Yet something

1

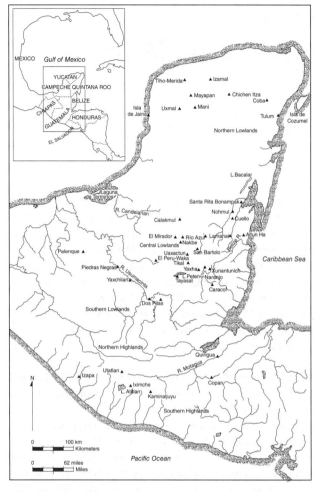

1. The Maya area.

definable, unique, and endlessly fascinating—what we call Maya culture—has clearly existed for millennia.

The Maya are therefore worth our attention for all these reasons and because they pose a riddle. Since Europeans appeared on their shores soon after 1500, Maya communities and their cultural traditions have suffered systematic destruction and oppression by outsiders. Yet in recent centuries, this outside world has devoted considerable attention to uncovering and understanding Maya civilization and history. As a result, the Maya are shrouded in mystery, an object of popular fascination, greatly misunderstood, and yet heavily studied.

Early in the emergence of the professional study of the Maya, scholars divided ancient Maya history (that is, Maya history before the arrival of Europeans) into three broad periods: the Preclassic (sometimes referred to as the Formative), the Classic, and the Postclassic. As the terminology implies, this classification was based on an evolutionary model that posited that the Classic period Maya were more sophisticated in terms of their culture, religion, and political system than the Maya who lived before and after. Within this model, the Preclassic period is understood as a time of foundational development and the Postclassic as a time of cultural decay. Modern research shows this model to be misguided. Some Mayanists now refer to the period more or less comprising the Preclassic and Classic as the *Mayacene*—the Maya-specific version of the global Early Anthropocene era of 3000 BCE to 1000 CE. Nonetheless, the traditional periodization of Maya history is a well-established custom, and we therefore outline it here.

Mayanists call their subjects *the Maya* or *the Mayas*, restricting the adjective *Mayan* to their languages. Those terms often require qualification because there are roughly thirty Maya ethnic groups. Therefore, where possible, Mayanists refer more specifically to ethnic groups, such as the Yucatec Maya or the Kaqchikel Maya,

3

Periods of Maya history

The major periods of ancient Maya history are typically subdivided into shorter periods, as shown here, along with approximate Western dates. We have added periods leading up to the present. Dates are CE unless otherwise indicated and are approximate, even when they appear specific (e.g., 825 or 1520), marking a point around which changes outweighed continuities.

Archaic period	8000–2000 BCE
Preclassic/Formative	2000–250 BCE
Early Preclassic	2000–1000 BCE
Middle Preclassic	1000–300 BCE
Late Preclassic	300 BCE–250 CE
Classic Period	250–950
Early Classic	250–600
Late Classic	600–825
Terminal Classic	825–950
Postclassic	950–1520
Early Postclassic	950–1250
Late Postclassic	1250–1520
Early Modern/Colonial	1520–1820
Contact/Conquest	1520–1550
Colonial	1550–1820
Modern	1820–present

or to larger groupings, such as the K'iche'an Maya or the Maya of Highland Guatemala.

All such groups are defined by their languages—that is, by the approximately thirty Mayan languages that survived into the modern period (there were likely more than thirty at the point of first contact with Spaniards). Most hieroglyphic inscriptions of the Classic period were probably in languages from the Choloid language group, primarily Classic Ch'olti'an, the ancestral language of today's Ch'orti' (now a tiny language area on the Guatemalan–Honduran border). The largest language area, with the most speakers historically and in the early twenty-first century, is the Yucatan Peninsula—not coincidentally the flattest region of the Maya world, with almost no mountains and rivers to divide people from each other; its Mayan language is Yukatek (we use the older, more common spelling of "Yucatec"), with a few other Yukatekan (Yucatecan) languages spoken at the peninsula's base (most notably Itzaj and Mopan).

Themes and mysteries

During the course of our chronological coverage of the cultural, political, and religious history of the Maya, we emphasize five themes. The first of these themes is Maya identity. The people we call Maya never thought of themselves as such. Before the broader application of the word starting in the nineteenth century, Maya was an obscure term restricted to a region of Yucatan. So what was the self-identity of the people we call Maya, how did Maya civilization come to be "invented," and why is that invention useful? As two archaeologists put it, the category of Maya is "a fiction from which deeper realities emerge."

The second theme is polity, or city-state political culture. If there was never a Maya Empire, despite the fact that Spanish colonists and modern scholars often claimed there had been, how were Maya polities conceived and constructed? What was daily life like both at the center and on the margins of those polities? For most of Maya history, those questions apply to the millennia before European contact. But they also apply to the centuries since contact, adjusted to the realities of multiple intrusions into the Maya world. For the early modern and modern periods, then, the

5

question becomes, How have Maya communities persisted—be they villages in regions where Mayas have lived for millennia or diasporic families far from the Maya area? The Maya have suffered numerous colonizations, yet their history in the postcontact era is not simply one of victimization; it is also the continuation of the precolonial Maya story of adaptation, survival, and the pursuit of local solutions.

The third theme is cosmovision and the world beyond. How did the Maya perceive the larger, outside world—ranging from foreign visitors and invaders to the supernatural and the celestial universe? Related to that theme is our fourth: artistic expression. How did the Maya reflect their world beliefs in the material objects they carved, painted, wrote, and built? One of the most alluring and captivating aspects of Maya civilization is its vibrantly visual nature. Is it fair to say that the Maya lived (and live) in a world of art?

Our fifth theme is that of Maya "mysteries"—not why the Maya are mysterious, but why have they been so widely perceived as such? There has long been a preoccupation in the West with the notion that Maya civilization is a riddle to be solved. The reasons for that perspective—part of what makes Maya history so compelling—all relate to the twin phenomena of disappearance and discovery. Beginning with Christopher Columbus in 1502, the ancient Maya have repeatedly been "discovered" by the West. The finding of the people and places of the Maya area, either living or long gone, continued with Spanish conquistadors, with the gentlemen-explorers of the nineteenth century, and with the pioneering archaeologists of modern Maya studies; it continues in the early twenty-first century with the sensationalization of new findings by each generation of Maya scholars.

Closely related is the belief that the Maya disappeared, taking their secret knowledge with them, an idea distorted and perpetuated by misunderstandings of scholarly theories on the phenomenon of "the Collapse" at the end of the Classic period. In the ninth and tenth centuries, city-states in the central region of the Maya area experienced changes that were, in some cases, sudden and dramatic. As a result, some abandoned cities remain deserted ruins (or partially restored tourist sites) to this day. But the Maya did not disappear and their civilization did not collapse. Likewise, in the sixteenth and seventeenth centuries, Spanish invasions and the spread of deadly diseases like smallpox (previously unknown in the Americas) caused kingdoms to collapse and populations to decline precipitously. But, again, Maya communities and cultures persisted.

More recently, "2012ology" stimulated interest in Maya civilization as a phenomenon of ancient mystery, a riddle ripe for rediscovery. "Predicted by the Mayans. Confirmed by science," ran one of the promotional blurbs for the movie *2012*: "Never before in history has a date been so significant to so many cultures, so many religions, scientists, and governments." The film did not take the topic too seriously; despite its high body count, it was "Old Testament–style destruction served with a smile" (as the *New York Times* put it). Yet while *2012* was more about the Hollywood genre of disaster movies than it was about Maya culture or ancient prophecies, the film nonetheless sought to capitalize on the widespread belief in this millennium's first decade that the ancient Maya had predicted the end of the world.

That belief was rooted in the fear that the advanced astronomical knowledge of the ancient Maya had allowed them to calculate that the apocalypse would occur on the date 13.0.0.0.0 in their calendar (our December 21, 2012). Although Mayanists insisted that the Maya had predicted no such thing, a veritable 2012ology industry spread rapidly into the tourism and entertainment industries, spawning films, books, websites, and cartoons by the thousands, all capitalizing on and perpetuating an unease regarding secret Maya knowledge and its potentially momentous mysteries.

The world did not end, of course, and neither have the Maya or the widespread fascination with their civilization. With Maya

2. This 2012 cartoon by Dan Piraro makes sense only if the reader knows that ancient Mayas supposedly predicted the world would end that year. Fears that the Maya were right were misguided but widespread.

communities historically subdivided in so many ways (geographical, linguistic, and chronological); with their very identity as a single people the invention of Mayanists (but appropriated by many Mayas today); and with their civilization so often seen as fundamentally mysterious, the pursuit of what made the Maya "the Maya" is all the more important.

Chapter 2
Maya genesis

The question of when the Maya became the Maya, from the archaeological perspective, will likely always be debated, as new evidence is uncovered and old evidence reinterpreted. But it is safe to outline broadly the gradual birth of the civilization we call *Maya*.

People began to settle the area around 9000 BCE; by 3000 BCE, maize farmers were clearing forest in the southern region, and in the second millennium BCE there is evidence of a widespread village culture gradually moving toward urbanism—as settlement became denser, for example, and public buildings such as ball courts became larger and more numerous. By the time of the first millennium BCE, if not before, the commonality and complexity of cultural practices across the Maya area—from art and architecture to agriculture and social structure—demonstrate that Maya civilization had been born.

With the escalation of urbanism during these Preclassic millennia, artistic, architectural, and knowledge production became more sophisticated. For example, upright stone shafts or stelae were erected in prominent urban locations, featuring carved and brightly colored portraits of rulers. As hieroglyphic script developed, stelae also included texts, helping these stone "canvases" to act as signposts and backdrops to performances, parades, and other political rituals. The increasingly elaborate nature of architectural complexes—a plethora of platforms, palaces, and pyramids—was made possible by ever more hierarchical social organization. The ruler of the city-state was at the apex of that hierarchy, and below him (or, on rare occasion, her) were lesser elites or nobles, followed by a merchant and artisanal class. Finally, there were families of farmers—the commoner majority—and, below them, slaves. By the closing centuries of the Preclassic period, there were six or seven layers to Maya society.

So how did the Maya themselves understand the genesis of their civilization? Like human societies the world over, the Maya did not share a common account of how the physical world and its inhabitants were created. In Maya art, architecture, and associated political organizations, tales of cosmogenesis were highly localized, all seeming to serve the political interests of each city-state's ruling elites. In many cases, Maya cities often proclaimed that the world and the deities responsible were created locally; no doubt a city's residents believed that the local patron deities were born in that city.

Our knowledge of ancient Maya mythistory—a complex blend of historical and mythological past events—comes from three primary kinds of evidentiary sources. Two predate European contact and one dates to the colonial period. The pre-Columbian sources come in the form of visual culture, such as painted ceramic vessels and walls, and hieroglyphic texts that adorn stelae, lintels, and the walls of monumental architectural features. Additionally, textual manuscripts from the colonial period, composed in various Mayan languages, contain detailed accounts of this ancient mythistory. All these sources can be tricky to interpret, but when they can be colluded, they underpin a strong argument for how the Maya viewed the supernatural creation of their world.

In their own words

By far the most detailed version of the Maya creation is found in the manuscript known as the *Popol Vuh*. Written in K'iche', one of highland Guatemala's Mayan languages, the manuscript survives in the early twenty-first century in Chicago's Newberry Library. Transcribed in 1701 or 1702 by a Dominican friar, Francisco Ximénez, the *Popol Vuh* was likely copied from an older K'iche' Mayan text that was composed at some point in the early colonial period. That earlier manuscript was likely redacted from a pre-Columbian codex that told the tale in both hieroglyphic text and image—but, unfortunately, Ximénez's version of the saga did not retain the ancient visual material.

The manuscript is divided roughly into three parts, perhaps reflecting its derivation from more than one pre-Columbian codex; its three parts reveal the political function of what is essentially a religious text. The first part is "cosmogonic"—it details the creation of the earth and the birthing of the gods, all directed by a pair of elderly deities, Tepeu and Gucumatz, labeled "the Makers." These beings created the terrestrial world, light, and eventually all of its animal inhabitants. The gods then wished to be venerated, so they began the process of what would become the ultimate creative act, the production of human beings. It took several tries to get it right. In their first attempt, the gods modeled humanoid beings out of mud and water, but these creatures simply melted away when exposed to rain. Next, they tried wood, crafting humanlike manikins, and while these were impervious to the elements, they were unable to speak and thus incapable of fulfilling their ritual obligations to the deities. They too were summarily destroyed, this time by a massive flood.

The second section of the *Popol Vuh* is the lengthiest and best known. It details the adventurous exploits of the Hero Twins, Hunahpu (One Hunter) and Xbalanque (Jaguar Deer). This portion begins a generation earlier, detailing the misadventures of the boys' father (Hun Hunahpu) and his own twin brother (Vucub Hunahpu). This first set of twins were avid ballplayers; their incessant bouncing of the heavy rubber ball on the ceiling of the Underworld came to disturb and upset the Lords of the Underworld who resided below, a level of the Maya cosmos called "Xibalba." The twins were summoned down to play ball with these Underworld gods and were eventually defeated. Hun Hunahpu's head was severed and hung in a cornfield.

The primary Lord of the Underworld had a beautiful daughter named Blood Moon, who heard about Hun Hunahpu's severed head and wished to see the curiosity for herself. She sneaked into the cornfield, where the head spoke to Blood Moon and spat into her palm—whereupon she found herself pregnant. Because pregnancy outside marriage was deemed socially improper, Blood Moon's father banished her to the terrestrial realm, sending his trusty owl to kill her. Instead, the owl let her go, fooling his master by returning with a ball of copal resin shaped in the form of a human heart to represent Blood Moon's vital organ.

Blood Moon found her way to the home of Hun Hunahpu, where she explained to his mother, Xmucané, that she was carrying her grandchildren, another set of boy twins. These children were born and grew up in the house of their grandmother, where their older half-brothers resided, another set of twins previously fathered by Hun Hunahpu. The older brothers were notoriously cruel to their younger siblings, who eventually outwitted them, transforming the older brothers into spider monkeys.

The Hero Twins' cunning and intelligence allowed them to manipulate their human and natural environments. But their true challenge came in their teen years, when they discovered their father and uncle's ball-game equipment, hidden in the rafters. Like their father and uncle, the Hero Twins became obsessed with the game, eventually catching the attention of the same Lords of

Xibalba who killed their father. Again, these twins were summoned by the Lords and were forced to endure a series of trials, all aimed at extinguishing the young Hero Twins. Time and time again, the boys outwitted the Underworld Lords, primarily by drawing on their own natural intelligence and knowledge of the natural world. Ultimately, they defeated the Lords of the Underworld.

The *Popol Vuh*'s final section is the shortest of the three. It details the last and successful attempt of the Makers to create human beings. This time, they were created from yellow and white cornmeal and were therefore capable of speech, movement, sight, and thought, all the elements necessary for the proper veneration of the deities. There then immediately emerged the lineages that controlled the K'iche' Maya during the Late Postclassic, into the colonial period, and right up to the moment of the manuscript's transcription at the turn of the eighteenth century. This reflected an ancient Maya tradition of directly linking ruling elites to cosmogonic narratives, thereby validating their political control.

Despite the mid–colonial period date of the extant *Popol Vuh* manuscript, an abundance of visual evidence suggests localized versions of this same tale circulated for at least two millennia. As early as the first millennium BCE, the Olmecs (whose civilization flourished west of the Maya area, before and during the Maya Preclassic period) placed stone representations of twin boys in sites such as La Venta. A little later, about 300 BCE, artists at the site of Izapa (in Chiapas) carved stelae to visualize pivotal moments of the narrative later recorded in the eighteenth century. And finally, Classic period painted ceramics provide an impressive corpus of related narrative scenes, produced throughout the Maya lowlands and beyond.

A popularly discussed ceramic vessel represents such an episode from early in the adventures of the Hero Twins: Hunahpu's shooting of Vucub Kaquix (Seven Macaw). In one rendering of

3. This polychrome plate represents a pivotal moment in the *Popol Vuh* when one of the Hero Twins, Hunahpu, shoots Vucub Kaquix as punishment for his egotism.

this event by an ancient Maya artist, we see the twins poised to shoot, blowguns protruding from their pursed lips. Seven Macaw is perched proudly, his resplendent feathers spread for all to see. According to the eighteenth-century manuscript, this early deity had become too confident for his own good; he believed his bejeweled teeth and eyes marked him as an equal to the sun. Hunahpu was instructed to bring him back down to size and did so by shooting him in the mouth, thereby knocking out his golden teeth. In the process, his lower jaw was shot off, forever explaining the atypical formation of the lower mandible of the macaw species.

This singular episode, which was important enough to be rendered by a courtly artist on one of the most elite art forms, serves as an example for the larger social function of Maya mythology in ancient society. Typically, these anecdotes have a moralizing character; in this example the lesson is not to prioritize one's individuality over the needs of the larger community. Additionally, these tales, in fashion similar to Rudyard Kipling's *Just So* stories of the late nineteenth century, enabled Maya people to easily explain the variation found in the natural world.

Nearly 1,000 years earlier, during the apex of the Classic period, Maya artists had similarly taken on the monumental recording of cosmogonic events, but utilizing an alternative approach and medium, the carving of stone hieroglyphic texts. Exemplified by a series of exceptional inscriptions from the center of Palenque, this technique involved the intricate carving from local basalt rock of hundreds of individual blocks of hieroglyphic text, arranged into panels. Examples of this form of recorded myth and history are scattered throughout the site but are especially well preserved in temples commissioned and funded under the realm of Palenque's thirteenth ruler, K'inich Kan Bahlam (r. 684–702).

In choosing this technique to detail local mythistory, K'inich Kan Bahlam was not attempting a break in regional practice; he was simply emulating the political strategies of his forebears. Following his father's death in 683 CE, K'inich Kan Bahlam embarked on an ambitious building program. The stunning result is known today as the Cross Group. Composed of three inward-facing mound-temple structures, this complex was conceived as a unified whole, with the architectural style and associated artwork together projecting a particular vision of K'inich Kan Bahlam's rule.

Atop each pyramid in Palenque, the typical temple form was laid out in stone. But within each temple was nestled an embedded secondary structure, a kind of interior sanctuary. These smaller spaces (the one in the Temple of the Cross is only two by three meters) housed large relief carvings, embedded in the backmost wall. The carved panels include both text and image, the figurative representations displaying K'inich Kan Bahlam interacting with various ancestors. What concerns us here is the hieroglyphic texts that speak to the creation of the patron deities of Palenque—archaeologists call them G1, G2, and G3—at the site of creation. The text labels the overall structure as "his [G1's] sweat bath." In the Maya world, semisubterranean sweat baths were used for a variety of medical and religious purposes, but perhaps most commonly to bring relief to women who were actively giving birth. Through this labeling, these structures and the sweat baths were thereby linked to divine birth and purification. The remainder of the hieroglyphic text provides a detailed genealogy of the Palenque dynasty, succinctly linking the city's human rulers to the lineage of the city's patron gods.

Further Classic period epigraphic evidence suggests that the Maya also maintained a distinct vision of how the physical world was established, an account that is slightly different than the one offered in the much later *Popol Vuh*. These glyphs speak of the setting up of the "three hearth stones of creation" at the starting date of the Maya calendrical system that scholars call the Long Count: August 11, 3114 BCE.

Finally, from the northern extreme of the Maya world, the Yucatan Peninsula, an additional account of creation exists, albeit not as lengthy or detailed as that in the *Popol Vuh*. Three versions are extant, in manuscripts known as the *Books of Chilam Balam* (the "Jaguar Priest"). These books were written alphabetically in Yucatec Maya in the colonial period, initially transcribed by Maya notaries from hieroglyphic books before they were lost or destroyed by Spanish priests. Copies differed from town to town, increasingly so over the colonial centuries—reflecting local lore, regional historical memory, the intrusion of Christian ideas, and varying interests in such topics as ancient prophecies, calendrical knowledge, and herbal cures. The three *Books of Chilam Balam* that contain accounts of the Maya cosmogenesis are in late colonial copies from the Yucatec towns of Chumayel, Tizimin, and Mani.

The current world order, according to the Jaguar Priest, was upset by a divine battle waged between two primary gods of the Postclassic pantheon, Oxlahuntiku ("He of the 13 Gods") and Bolontiku ("He of the 9 Gods"). These deities waged an epic battle against one another, and eventually Bolontiku emerged victorious, having ripped Oxlahuntiku to shreds and deposited his body throughout the world. Thereafter, a torrential flood wiped out all previous existence. As befitted Maya understandings of the life cycle, this destruction ushered in a new era of creation: five world trees were planted to raise the new sky, one in each of the cardinal directions, with a single tree in the center of the cosmos, holding aloft the celestial realm.

The archaeological evidence

Although the ancient Maya placed the creation of their society many millennia before our calendar's year zero, scholars recognize the emergence of a distinctly Maya culture during the Middle Preclassic period. This does not mean that humans had not inhabited the region previously. Excavations at sites such as Cuello have located archaeological features such as hard clay floors and postholes that date to around 1200 BCE, and other sites—Nakbe and Soconusco, for example—may be as old as 2000 BCE. In this very early period, referred to as the Archaic, people in the Maya region likely lived in nomadic bands that visited seasonal camps to procure food. The Archaic period is typically dated from 8000 BCE, but there were almost certainly people (pre-Mayas, if you like) living in, and moving through, the future Maya area for millennia before that.

Traditionally, the Early Preclassic has been determined as the moment when the first evidence of domesticated agriculture appears in the archaeological record, specifically the cultivation of corn. As with other human societies the world over, this agricultural development allowed for densely settled communities and eventually the emergence of social hierarchy. The early discovery of the "nixtamalization" (from the Nahuatl term *nextamalli*, derived from *nextli* ["cinders" or "ash"] and *tamalli* ["tamale"]) was also a boost to Mesoamerican societies. Mayas and other Mesoamericans began to soak and cook unhulled corn in an alkaline solution made from limewater or lye. In addition to making the corn tastier and easier to grind, this process allowed corn to provide dietary niacin, which, in combination with amino acids from cultivated beans, ensured a staple diet composed of a complete protein set.

Thus, by the Early Preclassic, settled villages peppered some regions of the Maya world—in the area around Soconusco, for example, where evidence for maize cultivation dates to circa 1700 BCE. Some scholars refer to these populations as the *Mokaya*. However, the highlands of Guatemala and the entirety of the lowlands (the Peten and the Yucatan) do not show as much evidence for this early cultural development; archaeologists have yet to determine exactly why this is the case. Regardless, the Early Preclassic villages of the Guatemalan and Chiapas coastal plains preserve remains of pole and thatch houses and a defined ceramic tradition, the Barra phase of 1900 to 1700 BCE. Mortuary practices begin to exhibit social differentiation in terms of included grave goods. For example, at El Vivero (in Chiapas) the burial of a young child included a difficult-to-procure and difficult-to-produce mica mirror, which adorned the child's forehead. These centuries also saw the earliest appearance of ceramic figurines with definable deities—such as the corn and rain gods—marking the origins of a defined Maya religion.

At the onset of the Middle Preclassic period around 1000 BCE, multiple settlements emerged, scattered throughout the Maya area. Most of these early villages (such as Cuello in Belize) were composed of simple clusters of house mounds, although archaeologists have been discovering that monumental architecture emerged early in the Middle Preclassic in a growing number of sites—such as Ceibal in the northern lowlands. By the end of the Middle Preclassic (300 BCE), towns scattered across the Maya area had embarked on monumental architectural development. The construction of larger and grander public structures, along with related material artifacts, ushered in the Late Preclassic period. The Late Preclassic was an era of

4. The Corn Deity receives the earth's bounty out of the mouth of an animated cave, as depicted in a scene from the north wall of the San Bartolo murals.

florescence, of growing social and cultural sophistication, as revealed by excavations at three important sites: Kaminaljuyu, partially buried underneath modern Guatemala City; San Bartolo, located in the Guatemalan lowlands; and El Mirador, situated in north Guatemala close to the Mexican border.

Kaminaljuyu has the earliest occupation history of the three; human settlement there dates to at least 1500 BCE. At that point, it was a mere village, but rapid urban development followed in the Late Preclassic years. Termed the "Miraflores" period by the site's earliest archaeologists, these years saw the building of a ceremonial core defined by mounds and plazas. Monumental artworks, such as stelae and altar/thrones, littered the site, many of which featured early hieroglyphic inscriptions. Evidence of such visual and spatial sophistication shows that a political and social hierarchy had become established in Kaminaljuyu, with an agricultural surplus capable of supporting full-time craftspeople, designers, architects, and the like. The city clearly exercised profound political, cultural, and economic influence over the Late Preclassic Maya world. For example, the hieroglyphic inscriptions and complex iconography of sculptures in Kaminaljuyu suggest that rulership was conceived as semidivine, premised on privileged access to deities and sacred knowledge. Such ideas would come to dominate political thinking in cities across the Maya area for many centuries to come.

Despite Kaminaljuyu's prominence in the Guatemalan highlands, the Maya lowlands were dominated politically by the largest site of the Late Preclassic period, El Mirador, located in northern Guatemala. In actuality, the El Mirador region hosted numerous Preclassic cities by 300 BCE, including Xulnal, Calakmul, Tintal, Waknal, and Nakbe. They constituted a political network that archaeologists have asserted was the first political and economic state in the Western Hemisphere.

Inhabited as early as the sixth century BCE, El Mirador reached its cultural apex around the fourth century BCE. The colossal city, the largest constructed in the pre-modern Western Hemisphere, eventually stretched an impressive thirty-eight square kilometers of monumental architecture by the Classic period. Here, all of the later hallmarks of Maya civilization were already in active use. For example, a regional network of causeways or raised roads (*sacbeob* in Yucatec, literally "white roads") linked El Mirador to other monumental cities in the region, while an active interregional trade network brought exotic goods such as shells from the Caribbean and Pacific, obsidian from the central highlands of Mexico, and jadeite from the Motagua River valley in southern Guatemala into the civic center to be used by families at the top of the social and political hierarchy. An extensive agricultural system that included raised fields (*chinampas*) helped to feed families in and around the city. And by this time, the Maya had a sophisticated understanding of mathematics, including the utilization of zero as a defined concept.

El Mirador is singularly impressive for the architectural and artistic sophistication of its earliest temple structures. The largest of these, "El Tigre" and "Danta," featured a triadic formation, composed of a monumental pyramidal base on which three distinct temples were built. This design is related to the mythological "three stones of creation," suggesting that cosmological concepts dictated architectural design in this early historical moment. The largest building, Danta, measures 600 by 330 meters at its base and stretches an impressive 72 meters into the sky, totaling approximately 2.8 million cubic meters of fill. Stuccoed and then painted a vibrant hue of red, these structures also featured complex architectural sculpture. Artists created three-dimensional sculptural reliefs, completed around 200 BCE, consisting of iconographic motifs such as jaguar paws and humanoid masks.

Perhaps the most impressive archaeological discovery of the early 2000s was archaeologist William Saturno's largely accidental finding of the painted walls of Structure 1 (commonly referred to as "Las Pinturas," or "The Paintings") at San Bartolo, Guatemala. Following subsequent field seasons of simultaneous excavation and conservation, the painted walls have been revealed. Their remarkably early date of 300 BCE turned Maya studies on its head, forcing scholars to reconsider the "dawn of the Maya" by about 200 years. The visual and technical sophistication of the wall paintings suggests a religion and associated ideological system that had been developing for decades prior to these paintings' production. Thus, what we had come to understand as distinctly and culturally Maya has now been pushed back earlier—and may need to be pushed earlier still.

Originally, the murals wrapped around the upper section of the small building's interior walls, but only the northern, western, and eastern sections have been preserved. The walls display elaborate mythological scenes, with deities and other forms rendered in hues of red and yellow and details enlivened in black. The scenes form a kind of continuous narrative, displaying moments of creation related to the enthronement of a ruler, similar but not identical to those described in the eighteenth-century *Popol Vuh*. The San Bartolo paintings revolve around biographical events of the Maize God; the various scenes' complexity and specificity demonstrate an elaborate and well-established mythological system.

In one scene, the Maize God receives gifts provided by a mythological motif that Mayanists refer to as "Flower Mountain." A serpent's body forms the composition's ground line, on which eight humanoid figures are rendered, and its gaping maw becomes the opening of a cave. Kneeling before the cave, a woman hands a male figure a vessel containing tamales. In turn, this male twists toward the largest figure in the composition, the Maize God, to hand him a flowering gourd plant. This primary figure then glances over his left shoulder to view two additional kneeling humans who have outstretched arms ready to receive the flowering gourd. Interestingly, this Maize God looks similar to earlier representations of a deity found in the Olmec region of the Gulf Coast, suggesting sustained cultural interaction between the Maya and their western coastal neighbors during the Preclassic period.

The presence of this scene in a minor temple dated to 300 BCE shows that the cultural traits that would come to define Classic period civilization were already well developed centuries before the supposed apex of Maya society. Although the juxtaposition of mythological history with archaeological evidence is a challenging but productive method for Mayanists working to better understand the genesis of the Maya, it is increasingly clear that early Maya history is exactly that: neither myth nor prehistory, but history, well supported by textual and material evidence.

Chapter 3
The divine king

On January 2, 695, a Maya prince named Waxaklajuun Ubaah K'awiil acceded to the throne of the powerful Maya polity of Copan. We shall call him 18-Rabbit, as archaeologists did for decades (although Mayanists now understand his name to mean "18 are the images of K'awiil"). Upon becoming the *ajaw*—the supreme lord or king (written *ahau* in the colonial period)—18-Rabbit directed his father's funerary rites, including the construction of an elaborate temple, known today as the Esmeralda Structure. During the next thirty-three years, 18-Rabbit would reign over a vast territory of vassal cities, oversee an intricate and sprawling trade network, and invest creative efforts on massive projects of urban renewal in his capital city. The Great Plaza typified these renovations; it was a ritual space that included seven larger-than-life portraits of him carved into splendid stone stelae.

But 18-Rabbit's energetic reign came to a dramatic end. Captured in warfare, the great king was ritually executed on May 3, 738, by the ruler of one of his dependent cities, K'ahk' Tiliw Chan Yopaat of Quirigua. His death brought to a close the half-millennium-long regional dominance of 18-Rabbit's lineage.

This microbiography of 18-Rabbit, one of the best understood *ajawtaak* or *ajawob* (plurals of *ajaw*), hints at the social,

5. An archaeologist rendered this fictive, but surprisingly accurate, rendering of Copán's ceremonial core; the spatial relationship between monumental plazas, soaring temple mounds, and the ball court is clearly shown.

political, and religious intricacies of ancient Maya culture—especially during the centuries of the Classic period (roughly 250 to 950). The development of Maya intellectual culture—its writing systems, mathematics, astronomy, and the production of sophisticated architectural structures and smaller-scale artworks such as painted pottery—was closely linked to the evolution of Maya rulership. As Maya society and its associated cultural traditions became increasingly complex during the course of the Classic centuries, rulership became associated with notions of divinity. Thus, 18-Rabbit was not just an *ajaw*; he was also a *k'uhul ajaw*, a "divine king." During the Classic period, Maya rulers were often divine kings, genetically related to the deities who created the universe, from whom they directly traced their lineage. They were understood to control the natural and supernatural world on which human survival depended.

Cities, royal centers, and dynasties

We are able to date major events in the lives of Maya monarchs and other elites with great precision—often to the very day. How is that possible? It is because of the combination of the calendrical and writing systems developed by Mayas in the Late Preclassic period (300 BCE–250 CE), in particular the written use of the calendar that we call the Long Count.

The appearance of Long Count dates on monuments in the third century CE is one of the key cultural developments defining the onset of the Classic era. Although it has been used as the defining feature of the Classic era, it is now widely accepted that the calendar had been in use for centuries, perhaps even as early as the first century BCE, at the start of the Late Preclassic (Maya carvers inscribed Stela 2 at the site of Chiapa de Corzo with a date corresponding to 36 BCE). Regardless of this early appearance, widespread use of Long Count dates on public monuments ushers in the Classic period.

This linear system of time reckoning is based on a 360-day "year" and has a start date of 14 August 3114 BCE. Scholars have been unable to determine exactly what the Maya believed to have occurred on that primordial date, which predates the emergence of Maya society. Time marched forward from the start date in 3114 BCE, based on the foundational unit of time, the *k'in*. From the Maya perspective, the *k'in* was calculated as the amount of time it took for the sun to cycle around the earth (twenty-four hours, or a single day). The Long Count of days was calculated from a series of temporal cycles, each one longer than the other—twenty *k'ins* equaled a *winal*, eighteen *winals* composed a *tun* (360 days), twenty *tuns* completed a *k'atun* (7,200 days), and twenty *k'atuns* equaled a *bak'tun* (144,000 days). More rarely, the Maya recorded impossibly long cycles of time, such as the mega *alawtun*, consisting of 23 million days.

The Maya calendar and the end of the world

The sophistication of the ancient Maya calendar, combined with the West's deep-rooted association of the Maya with mysterious endings, underpinned 2012ology, a phenomenon that manifested on a worldwide scale leading up to a supposed apocalypse prophesied by Mayas.

Mayanist scholars unwittingly planted the seeds from which 2012ology grew by suggesting that the multiple vigesimal places of the Maya Long Count created ominous turning points every 400 years—just as the decimal places of our calendar make century and millennium beginnings and endings significant to us. The ancient Maya lived in the Long Count era of thirteen cycles of 400 years, stretching from August 14, 3114 BCE, to December 21, 2012 CE (both 13.0.0.0.0). What if, scholars idly speculated, Maya priests imagined the great cycle ending would mark the end of the present universe?

In 1996, a preliminary reading of a glyphic text from the small site of Tortuguero was posted online, citing the date 13.0.0.0.0 as the time when "blackness will occur." That was interpreted as a prophecy of doom, although the original epigraphers soon posted a retraction. As 2012 approached, scholars explained that the Tortuguero glyphs recorded a building dedication text, not a prophecy, and that Western—not Maya—civilization had been preoccupied with apocalypse for two millennia. In the sixteenth century, Franciscan missionaries filled with millennarian fervor came to the colonies that conquistadors had established among the Maya, convinced that indigenous conversion to Christianity was an urgent prerequisite to the Second Coming of Christ. Some elements of Franciscan apocalyptic ideology were absorbed by the Maya elite, most notably in Yucatan, and incorporated into colonial-era literature such as the *Books of Chilam Balam*. Centuries later, 2012ologists would take such texts as evidence of Maya apocalypticism, just as they misappropriated the Tortuguero glyphic text.

Maya artists typically created a vertical column of numbers attached to a hieroglyph that signified the Long Count's internal divisions. For example, a date corresponding to our calendar's 637 CE would be recorded as 9.10.5.0.0, or nine *bak'tuns* (1,296,000 days), ten *k'atuns* (72,000 days), five *tuns* (1,800 days), zero *winals*, and zero *k'ins* since 3114 BCE. This linear temporal system allowed scholars to make a correlation with our own calendar, granting the Classic Maya a chartable and chronologically based "history" impossible for other Amerindian groups.

Along with the Long Count's linear reckoning of time, the Maya (along with most Mesoamerican cultures) observed a cyclical calendar known to us as the "Calendar Round." Like the Long Count, the Calendar Round was internally divided; its two day counts were called the *tzolk'in* and the *haab'*. The *tzolk'in* was composed of 13 day numbers paired with 20 day names (1 Muluk through 13 Muluk, 1 Ok through 13 Ok, and so on) to total 260 days. The *haab'* was longer, comprising 365 days broken down into 18 months of 20 days each and a single month of 5 days. These calendars ran concurrently, so to arrive on the same combination of *tzolk'in* number/day name and a specific day in the *haab'* required the passage of 18,980 days, or 52 years. Like visual renderings of the Long Count, Maya artists and scribes recorded Calendar Round dates using a combination of numerical signifiers attached to glyphs that referenced the various day and month names.

The calendrical milestones noted in Classic-era texts were highly varied; along with the thousands of other Maya texts, carvings, and artifacts, calendrical records reveal a civilization *not* preoccupied with the end of the world. Instead, ancient Mayas were interested in fertility and growth, with the cycles of life and agriculture; in time, its measurement, and its constancy; in the permanence of place and the deep-rootedness of local identities; and in the ways in which the natural and supernatural worlds interfaced and dovetailed, forming a single world of people and animals, ancestors, and deities.

By the third century CE, the onset of the Classic era, we can speak of fully formed Maya polities (some would say city-states). Each powerful polity was demarcated by a single capital city and a network of dependent towns and villages that were in a defined economic relationship with the primary city—such as that of Copan and Quirigua. Central to that economic relationship was the expectation that capital cities would receive tribute payments in the form of cultivated foodstuffs, crafted goods, and labor. In return, subject towns were protected from starvation and external attack, thereby forging a reciprocal bond between center and periphery. That bond was expressed and understood as a sacred one, safeguarded by the capital's divine king.

Cultural traits that defined the Preclassic became increasingly complex in the Classic period. Architectural innovations became standardized, the best example of which is the stone corbeled vault, a modified arch composed of in-stepping rectilinear blocks. Maya architects used corbeled vaults exclusively to create interior space in domestic, administrative, and religious structures, such as the small temples that were placed atop pyramids; as pyramids grew taller, architects turned more and more to corbeled vaults and plastered, painted roof combs to make those temples bigger (or at least to make them seem bigger) inside and out. Earlier city plans were reconstructed according to the whims and tastes of reigning kings, often resulting in increasingly standardized and ordered spaces—such as airy, open plazas surrounded on all four sides by monumental buildings. The few architectural paintings that survived the tropical climate reveal artists experimenting with innovative pigments, crowded compositions, and systems of representation, such as naturalized human forms. At the same time, and perhaps most important for Maya historians, hieroglyphic writing reached its most elaborate form in these centuries.

The best known sites—such as Copan, Tikal, Calakmul, and Palenque—all date to this era. The purpose of all these buildings, monuments, carved dates, written texts, and painted walls was to glorify the capital city and its ruling dynasty—above all, the personification of state and dynasty in the form of the ruling divine king. City-state and dynasty were intertwined, defining each other. At the time of contact with Europeans, many kingdoms were named after their ruling dynasties. In northern Yucatan, Ceh Pech and Can Pech were both named for the royal family of Pech; Tutul Xiu and Cupul were named after their rulers; and Ah Kin Chel and Chikinchel loosely referred to the kingdoms of the Priest Chel and the Western Chel. The kingdom that dominated the southern lowlands from the Late Postclassic to 1697 was called Peten Itza or Tah Itza, which could be translated as the Kingdom of the Itza or Itzaland. We now know that the pattern was a tradition going back at least a millennium: in those same southern lowlands, a millennium earlier, the kingdom centered on Caracol was named Kaanul, after its divine kings, the same lineage name used for a Yucatec state (Canul, in colonial orthography) at the time of contact.

Features of urban design—such as corbeled vaults, stepped pyramids, ball courts, palace complexes, and plazas—make cities of the area recognizably Maya, although they were built across thousands of years or thousands of years apart. And yet no two Maya cities are identical. Each one bears witness to the possibilities and limitations of its regional environment and to the local priorities and individual inspirations of its rulers, architects, and artists.

The Teotihuacan factor

One of the themes of Maya history is the regular intrusion into the Maya area of peoples from the west (especially from what we call central Mexico). Indeed, the earliest settlers in the Maya area migrated from that direction and, ever since, people periodically came into Maya lands—whether temporarily as traders, peacefully as refugees, or aggressively as part of an invading army. That fact should not be misread, however, as meaning that the Maya were "foreign" or easily conquered or that their civilization was imported. On the contrary, Maya civilization was autochthonous, locally developed and distinct from the cultures to its west and east; but it was certainly influenced by peoples, cultures, and material objects that came from outside and were thereby absorbed into the Maya world and became part of that process of civilizational development.

One of the most important examples of such contact took place in the fourth century. The central Mexican metropolis of Teotihuacan emerged at the turn of the millennium (that is, around the year 0) as a powerful regional player, expanding over the next six centuries to become the greatest urban center yet built in the Americas. More than 100,000 inhabitants, perhaps even twice that many, lived in well-ordered neighborhoods covering a dozen square miles, centered on massive avenues and pyramids that are still standing in the early twenty-first century (one of Mexico's top tourist attractions). The extent of Teotihuacan's empire is not known, but clues lie in its size, its wealth, and the militarism of its monumental art. Furthermore, many of the stylistic features of that art began to appear in the Maya world in the fourth century.

In some cases, the nature of the relationship between Teotihuacan and Maya cities appears to have been largely economic and diplomatic. Soon after 400 CE, many of the city-states of highland Guatemala created alliances with Teotihuacan, perhaps even becoming economic partners, with the southern Maya cities functioning as trading enclaves for the northern metropolis. Archaeologically, this cultural contact is clearly reflected in the sudden shift in architecture at cities such as Kaminaljuyu. Most obviously, the monumental architecture of this period (called "Esperanza" by Mayanists) reflects a hybridization of Maya and

Teotihuacan traditions, with Maya architects and stonemasons appropriating the diagnostic *talud/tablero* style from the northern empire. The structures of the site's acropolis, for example, feature increasingly smaller terraces as the building reaches upward, composed of varying flat panels (the *tablero*) superimposed by inward slanting planes (the *talud*). In addition, two burials at Kaminaljuyu included ceramic vessels rendered in an unmistakable central Mexican style and color scheme, using a specific plaster technique and featuring attributes of deities local to Teotihuacan—such as the storm deity whom the Aztecs would a thousand years later call "Tlaloc."

A contrasting story of cultural contact played out in the north, in the Peten cities of Tikal, Uaxactun, and La Sufricaya, where another hybrid Teotihuacan–Maya culture (sometimes dubbed Tzak'ol after its ceramics) flourished in the late fourth through early sixth centuries. Its initiation can be given a specific date: January 16, 378, when Chak Tok Ich'aak I ("Great Jaguar Paw"), the eighth *ajaw* of the dynasty that had ruled Tikal since the first century, died. His death was surely a violent one, because on the same day, Sihyaj K'ahk' ("Fire is Born") "arrived," according to two stelae from neighboring Uaxactun. This pivotal historical event is also described on Tikal's Stela 31. Sihyaj K'ahk' soon installed on Tikal's throne a new ruler, Yax Nuun Ahiin. Stela 4 is a portrait that commemorates the accession of the new ruler; the carving images him facing frontally, as was customary in Teotihuacan, surrounded by other central Mexican icons, such as a pectin shell necklace and a representation of the central Mexican rain deity, while at the same time incorporating local Maya motifs, such as the Jaguar Deity of the Underworld.

Some archaeologists have speculated that this boy-ruler, Yax Nuun Ahiin ("First Crocodile," aka "Curl Nose"), was a son of the distant emperor in Teotihuacan. Whether that is true or not, he began a dynasty that ruled Tikal for almost two centuries. Other neighboring urban centers also seem to have accepted rulers associated with Teotihuacan—most notably Tikal's near neighbor to the north, Uaxactun—and there is abundant evidence of a strong flow of trade goods between central Mexico and the central Maya region during these Early Classic centuries. Teotihuacan's influence, and perhaps political dominance of some kind, even extended north into the Yucatan—as shown in Early Classic stone carvings and other evidence from sites in the peninsula's Puuc region.

The political and cultural reach of Teotihuacan also extended farther south and east, as far as the city of Copan. There, in 426, a new dynasty was founded by K'inich Yax K'uk' Mo' ("Great Sun Quetzal Macaw"), who had also arrived from the west. Because archaeologists have excavated his tomb and that of his widow, and because he was celebrated on monuments and texts commissioned by his successors, we know that Yax K'uk' Mo' had close ties to Teotihuacan. He may even have ruled as a royal representative of that empire. But bone chemistry shows that he grew up in the Maya heartland of the Peten, in or near Tikal, and the dynasty he founded was Maya, not Teotihuacano—indeed, he initiated one of the great divine dynasties of Maya history, whose sixteen successive *k'uhul ajawtaak* ruled Copan through to 820.

If Copan's ties to Teotihuacan were indirect, the Peten–Teotihuacan connection seems to have been more direct, and it was thus severed as the empire faltered in the sixth century. It is unclear which of these two events was cause and which effect: a city-state allied to Tikal, Caracol, switched sides to join a regional rival of Tikal's, Calakmul, and to attack and sack Tikal in 562; meanwhile, Teotihuacan's imperial power was waning, and by century's end that capital city itself had been sacked.

Maya warfare

We should not misread the importance of Teotihuacan in Early Classic Maya history to imagine that invaders from central Mexico introduced warfare to peace-loving Mayas. Yet such misinterpretations can be found in many old textbooks: for much of the twentieth century, Mayanist scholars imagined Maya rulers as stargazing priest-kings who seldom, if ever, started wars. But with the decipherment of glyphs in the second half of the twentieth century, the accepted opinion on Maya warfare was completely reversed. It is now understood that the Maya waged war no less (but also no more) than other societies. Indeed, one expression of the importance of kings is the pattern of warfare in the Maya world.

To some extent, warfare was a part of Maya life; that is, while most Mayas lived in peace most of the time, it is unlikely that a Maya man or woman could live to old age without experiencing or witnessing warfare. Mayas went to war with a primary goal: to capture. Glyphic inscriptions record victory when an enemy king or war captain was "seized" (*chuhkaj*). Success in war was also marked by the taking or "bringing down of enemy shields and flint weapons" (*jubuy utook' upakal*), by "the burning" (*puluy*) of city centers, and by the smashing and burying of monuments. War captives were treated variously, but always with ritual and ceremony—because Maya warfare was a highly orchestrated affair, from its elaborate costumes to its martial music, from its prebattle preparations to its postwar executions and commemorations. Captives were sometimes tortured (as in the murals at Bonampak, depicting war prisoners whose nails have just been extracted), possibly forced to play a ball game with their death as a predetermined outcome, or stripped and decorated with paper in preparation for public decapitation. In the evocative phrasing of an inscription used in multiple sites, at times "the blood pooled, the heads piled up."

Warfare divided Mayas against each other in obvious ways, but it also tied them together. Take, for example, the two kingdoms of Piedras Negras and Yaxchilan, both located on the Usumacinta River (which serves as a border between Guatemala and Mexico in

6. In an encompassing view of a polychrome cylindrical vase, victorious Maya warriors display their prisoners of war in a public procession.

the early twenty-first century). Divine king culture reached the region in the fourth century; the dynasty that would rule Yaxchilan during the Classic centuries, for example, claimed to found the city in 359. For the next 450 years, Yaxchilan developed complex relations of trade, intermarriage, and periodic armed conflict with its neighbors, especially Piedras Negras—some thirty miles downriver.

In the closing decades of the seventh century, Piedras Negras had the regional upper hand, and Yaxchilan's king, Shield Jaguar III, was subordinate to the dominant city's *k'uhul ajaw*. But this was also a time of population growth, adding conflict over access to land to the traditional competition of trade route control. As a result, during the eighth century, the two city-states built between them a fortified frontier of new border towns and defensive walls. The frontier was then extended into the valley on what is today the Mexican side of the river, where smaller city-states were coopted or forced into acting as frontier sites defending the interests of Piedras Negras or Yaxchilan.

Shield Jaguar III was succeeded in 742 by a ruler so subordinate to the king of Piedras Negras that we know of his existence only from a monument in that city, recording the Yaxchilan ruler's presence as a tributary visitor or perhaps a hostage. Then, in 752, a son of Shield Jaguar III took to the throne of Yaxchilan as Bird Jaguar IV. He destroyed almost all records of his shameful predecessor's rule, strengthened Yaxchilan's frontier against Piedras Negras, and initiated decades of warfare against the powerful neighbor—culminating in the capture of its king by Yaxchilan's king, Tatbu Skull III, in 808, and the sacking of Piedras Negras a few years later.

One might expect that such a victory would usher in an age of peace-based regional dominance for Yaxchilan and glory for its divine dynasty. And indeed, the frontier fortifications seem to have been abandoned, and their towns went into decline. But the factors that provoked the war, such as increased pressure on the land, appear to have combined with the disruptive effect of warfare to undermine the authority of the king system itself. The captured king of Piedras Negras was that city's last *k'uhul ajaw* to be immortalized on a monument, but Tatbu Skull III also proved to be Yaxchilan's last *k'uhul ajaw*. The region was far from abandoned, but Yaxchilan lost its clout as a ceremonial political center. Without war to fuel its regional dominance, the city withered away and people dispersed across the landscape.

Regional warfare, then, in the form of controlled violent rivalry between neighboring city-states, was driven by and sustained the divine king system. It helped bind regions together during the Classic—until it conspired to bring the era of divine kings to a close. It is not coincidental that in the central Maya area, where Classic-era polities flourished most spectacularly, two periods of intense warfare marked the rise and fall of Classic divine king political culture: one in the third century and the other in the ninth and tenth centuries.

Divine queens

The history of the ruling class of the ancient Maya may have been dominated by men, but Maya women embodied political and religious roles as well. The decipherment of hieroglyphs helped reveal these historical actors. In fact, with each new discovery by scholars of another high-ranking female ruler, we are arguably closer to being obliged to talk about divine monarchy rather than divine kingship.

One example of a divine queen was Lady K'abel ("Waterlily-Hand"), a member of the Kaanul or Snake Dynasty that ruled Calakmul, the capital city of the family's regional empire. A carved portrait of her survived (Figure 7, numbered Stela 34 by archaeologists). Although the piece was looted, and therefore damaged, before Mayanists could study it, its legible glyphs have allowed epigraphers to identify its origins (often not the case with looted objects).

Lady K'abel married K'inich Bahlam II, a man of a lesser status, but from a local noble family. Together they politically dominated one of Calakmul's vassal towns, El Perú-Waka'. Hieroglyphic inscriptions, such as that in her portrait, refer to Lady K'abel with the title of *Ix Kaloomte'* ("Lady Supreme Warlord"), the highest royal rank (to date, five other Maya queens have been identified with this title). The inclusion of this particular appellation caused some archaeologists to speculate that this queen might have led warriors into battle against Calakmul's chief rival, Tikal.

Having died sometime between 702 and 711, Lady K'abel was interred in the city's largest pyramid mound (Structure M13-1), inside a masonry crypt with dozens of elite grave goods, including worked jade pieces, multiple pieces of elaborately decorated pottery, and a ceramic plate painted to resemble a warrior's shield. Perhaps the greatest testament to Lady K'abel's legacy is the fact that for two centuries after her death, Maya petitioners offered crafted trinkets, whistles, shells, and the like, creating a shrine at their queen's final resting place.

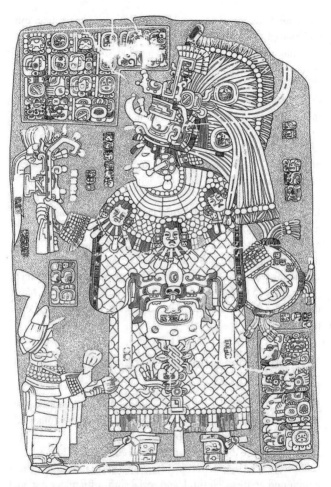

7. This stela, dated to 692 CE, features Lady K'abel of the Kaanul dynasty, ruler of El Perú-Waka' in the late seventh century. It was originally paired with another stela that depicted her husband. The two monumental sculptures were erected in front of a monumental pyramid mound as a form of royal portraiture.

Although Lady K'abel was not local to El Perú-Waka', iconographic and hieroglyphic evidence suggests that she outranked her husband. In fact, her status may in part have been rooted in her nonlocal origins, allowing her to cement a Calakmul–El Perú-Waka' alliance. Not only did she alone maintain the *Ix Kaloomte'* title, but also, her husband's portrait stela, which originally stood in the city's main plaza next to her own, was not carved with the same level of three-dimensionality, allowing Lady K'abel's representation to maintain visual prominence. She alone is attended by her palace dwarf and wears the lattice-beaded jade dress diagnostic of the male maize deity.

Lady K'abel's costume choice correlates well with our larger understanding of how the Maya saw men and women in complementary roles; both maleness and femaleness were necessary for rituals to be effective and ceremonies to be complete. If this was widely true of political and religious ritual, it may have generally been true of rulership in Maya royal centers. If so, Maya monarchies featured an interdependency, not a hierarchy, of kings and queens.

The end of the world, part I: the Classic period's "Collapse"

Following about eight centuries of cultural development, the Maya world experienced what has popularly been called "the Collapse." The phrase is still used, even by some Mayanists, but most scholars now see it as a misnomer. Maya civilization did not collapse, but underwent a transition, more accurately described as a profound political, cultural, and social shift, with major regional variations.

What exactly happened at the end of the Classic era that led modern people to assume the occurrence of a civilizational collapse? In the ninth and tenth centuries, the political system of the *k'uhul ajaw* declined and ended, along with the religious, visual, and intellectual cultures that sustained it—such as the use of the Long Count calendar and the erection of monumental stelae. At the same time, the population of some kingdoms declined. For residents of some states, the change was negative, dramatic, and rapid—a combination of warfare and famine, for example, that upended the fortunes of a kingdom within years, if not months, and resulted in a site's permanent desertion. Many of the cities that had flourished as vast and splendid Classic-era capitals—such as Palenque, Tikal, and Copan—were abandoned or their central structures ceased to be maintained or replaced.

The structural cause or root of this crisis seems to have been the *k'uhul ajaw* cult itself. The glorification of dynasty and authority by divine rulers encouraged ambitious building schemes and aggressive regional expansion, leading to population growth and increased demand for food, tribute goods, and trade products. No one kingdom could establish imperial hegemony over most of the Maya area, because—ironically—the *k'uhul ajaw* cult permeated every polity, stimulating long-term regional rivalries between city-states and rebellions by subject ones. As land use became more intensive, environmental degradation reduced agrarian production, thereby increasing the likelihood of famine, migration, warfare, and regional or internal revolt. Those factors, acting as proximate causes of collapse, led to city-state failure, the abandonment of city centers, and the rejection of *k'uhul ajawob*.

What did not happen was the failure of polities or population decline in all regions of the Maya world; Maya civilization did not cease, nor did it experience a sudden, dramatic, or traumatic transformation. An appreciation of regional variation, then, is crucial to understanding the gradual shift from the Classic era to the Postclassic. The challenges of the ninth and tenth centuries—a sustained drought in the early tenth century, the deterioration of the Maya relationship to their agricultural and other resources, the destabilizing impact of warfare and competition between city-states, and disenchantment with the ideology and institution of divine kingship—were experienced differently by Maya families in each region, even by each kingdom.

For example, for much of the eighth century the kingdom of Dos Pilas and its *k'uhul ajaw* controlled the entire Petexbatun region (in the southwest Peten). But in 760, the subject city of Tamarindito rebelled, attacked, and sacked Dos Pilas. Although other regional cities must have joined Tamarindito, it was not able to establish local domination, leading to a century of regional warfare. Surviving cities and towns became highly fortified, people fled, and the population rapidly declined.

In contrast, the decline of Tikal and Copan was more gradual. In many ways, both kingdoms were at their peak in the eighth century; then in the ninth their regional reach fragmented, the kingship cult faded, and the era of monumental construction ended. Yet the cities were not abandoned. Maya families continued to live, farm, and hunt in and around the great palaces and pyramids, even if they let the rainforest rapidly encroach on their walls and slowly pull the stones apart.

In even greater contrast, other kingdoms experienced a cultural and political florescence during the ninth and tenth centuries. Lamanai, for example, in what is today northern Belize, continued to prosper and even seems to have grown—perhaps receiving refugees from less fortunate regions. Like other city-states in Belize and eastern Yucatan, it was still occupied when Spaniards arrived in the sixteenth century. Further north in the Yucatan Peninsula, cities like Uxmal, Ek Balam, Coba, and Chichén Itzá experienced major population surges and corresponding alterations of their urban landscapes. In the closing centuries of the Classic (the Terminal Classic, as archaeologists call it) and in the Postclassic era, city-states and kingdoms in Yucatan developed new regional artistic and architectural styles. As with the Classic-era kingdoms of the central and southern regions, such expressions of cultural vitality reflected a mixture of local development, the influence of migrating people and ideas from within the greater Maya area, and the impact of increased and multidirectional contact with adjacent polities and cultures—particularly those of central Mexico.

In the early twenty-first century, the most visited ancient Maya city is Chichén Itzá. Its heyday was the tenth to thirteenth centuries—hundreds of years after the Collapse. It should be clear, then, to the busloads of tourists who are disgorged into the site daily, as well as to anyone interested in but not fortunate enough to tour those ruins, that the end of the Classic period in Maya history was not the end of the Maya world.

But the very nature of Chichén Itzá today—an open-air museum of partially reconstructed masonry structures devoid of color, with highlights like the great *cenote*, the ball court, and the temples presented in terms of "human sacrifice"—suggests disappearance. The place itself proves to visitors what their tour guides or guidebooks (or smartphone apps) tend to claim: If the Collapse did not completely wipe out the ancient Maya, the Spanish conquistadors finished the job, or the modern world swept them away. The barren nature of the site leaves visitors to ponder, How could ancient peoples have supported urban areas where only a few farmers eke out a living today?

That, at least, is how the non-Mayanist scholar Jared Diamond approaches the topic in *Collapse: How Societies Choose to Fail or Succeed*. His rationale for including the Maya in his book is that "the Maya cities impress us not only with that mystery"—referring to the question just posed—"and with their beauty," but also because they are "depopulated." Yet an understanding of the Maya area as a whole reveals that the Postclassic era—the period from the end of the Classic era to the arrival of Europeans—was long and complex. The beginning and end of that period were also more gradual than is suggested by the precise dates—950 and 1520—typically given it (including by us). Above all, the

41

transitions surrounding 950 and starting around 1520 remain controversial for the way in which they have been represented as marking an end to Maya civilization. While the Classic era, the age of the divine kings and queens, was indeed a golden age of Maya politics and culture, the Maya never met a mysterious end—either at the time of so-called Collapse or later, at the time of the so-called Spanish Conquest.

Chapter 4
The writing rabbit

Art was not simply a part of Maya culture or just the way that the elite or ruling class visually expressed their privileged position. Art was central to how the Maya conceived of their world and how they lived in it. Art in numerous forms—the built environment, sculpture, carving and painting, writing, dress and jewelry, ceramics, toys, and so on—surrounded the residents and visitors to the thousands of cities and towns that studded the region.

Thus, the residents of Maya city-states and villages memorialized cultural values and gave them permanent form in artifacts, from small ceramic figurines to monumental pyramid mounds. Those artifacts told Maya individuals about themselves—who they were and where they lived. Although only a fraction of the Maya visual world survived the ravages of time, climate, and human intervention, what does remain reveals a sophisticated aesthetic defined by subtle localization—because objects were site-specific and defined by regional styles.

Art-script-creators

There is no term in Mayan languages that is an exact cognate for *art*. This may be because what we think of as art was ubiquitous in Maya homes and neighborhoods, where stucco, paint, and carved designs turned everyday objects and surfaces into characteristically Maya artwork. There were, however, precise terms for the numerous specific art forms that they developed—be it on a low bowl (*lak*) or cylindrical vessel (*uk'ib* or *uch'ib*) or on the face of a funerary pyramid (*muhknal*) or stone monument (*lakamtuun*).

Tellingly, there was also a single term for a painter and writer (*aj tz'ihb*, an "art-script-creator"). In many cases, *aj tz'ihbob* proudly signed their names on their creations, as with Stela 34 from El Perú-Waka' (Figure 7), on which eleven artist signatures have been identified. These artist-scribes were sometimes represented in Classic period images as the craftiest of animals, such as deer or monkeys. On one ceramic vessel (Figure 8), the *aj tz'ihb* is a rabbit, sitting at the base of an enthroned Lord of the Underworld, his pen poised above an accordion-folded manuscript covered in jaguar fur, ready to write or draw. (Because the vessel was looted, its city-state origin is unknown.)

From such mythical scenes, we know that elite artists were part of Maya courtly life; their workshops have been located and excavated in close proximity to royal palaces in cities such as Copan and Palenque. Moreover, artists frequently worked in more than one medium. Stylistic markers and artist signatures reveal that skilled carvers often worked on both stone monuments and

8. On this vessel, a small rabbit, presumably a metaphor for a human artist-scribe, composes an accordion-folded codex.

pottery, while some painter-scribes could move between codices and ceramics—particularly codex-style ceramics, such as vessels (for example, Figure 8) where the painting style emulates that of painting on fig-bark paper.

Maya art had multiple social purposes, as reflected in its aesthetic and technical diversity. We may never understand the full functional range of Maya creative activities because a great deal of art on nondurable materials—such as paper and textiles—must have perished. Consequently, our grasp of nonelite artistic practices and traditions is limited. But at the highest echelons of Maya society and on a general level, it is clear that visual production was intended to lend ideological support to ruling lineages. Both small-scale and monumental art served to buttress claims of authority by visually and publicly advertising the *k'uhul ajaw* and his family's status, which was usually linked to a privileged relationship with the supernatural world of the deities. This favored position allowed ruling lineages to claim further control over those aspects of the natural and human worlds that dictated the survivability of their entire community—such as rainfall, the changing of the seasons, and success in warfare.

Crucial to this relationship was the charting of cosmic and mundane time (human history), which was possible only because of the development of a complex writing system. Hieroglyphic writing has rightly underpinned a great deal of the scholarly and popular interest in the ancient Maya, helping to create over the past century and a half the Maya mystique—that perception of Maya civilization as a mystery or riddle to be solved. The Maya left thousands of glyphic texts; their script may have been the most complex form of writing ever devised in antiquity (Mayanists certainly believe so). By the time of European contact in the sixteenth century, its use may have declined, but the notion— commonly believed in the nineteenth and twentieth centuries, including by Mayanists—that glyphic literacy and book production had almost completely ceased before contact is surely false. It was more likely the violent suppression of glyphic writing by Spanish friars that terminated the tradition during the colonial period. Either way, the ability to read the beautiful symbols was lost.

Early Mayanists began the modern campaign to "break the Maya code" in the nineteenth century, but their efforts were stymied by failures and disagreements, and they did not produce a sustained breakthrough until the closing decades of the twentieth century. When the breakthrough came, the result was spectacular. With the code broken, epigraphers were able to read thousands of texts, thereby dramatically overturning and deepening our understanding of Maya civilization. By the turn of the twenty-first century, professional and amateur Mayanists alike were achieving new insights at a dizzying pace, and by the century's third decade the discovery and decipherment of the vast extant corpus of glyphs reached (by most estimates) the 90 percent mark.

That dramatic story begs two core questions. First, what form did Maya hieroglyphic writing take for it to be both so expressive and so difficult for modern scholars to decipher? The answer is deceptively simple: it was logophonetic. The term means a combination of logographic—that is, hieroglyphs often contain logograms, signs that represent whole words or parts of words— and phonetic. As is the case with most logophonetic scripts, the phonetic component does not reduce the phonemes or sounds of the language to their smallest possible component (as in the letters of the Roman alphabet), but instead records them as syllables—a consonant plus a vowel (CV). To write glyphically a word that ended in a consonant (say, a CVC word), Maya scribes would use two syllables (CV-CV), relying on readers to understand that the final vowel was to be ignored. Any ambiguity could be reduced by adding a logogram, usually attached to—and thus part of—the same glyph. For literate Maya, the complexity of the system not only facilitated clear communication of information, but also permitted nuance, allusion, innuendo, and numerous

Code-breaking

The story of the decipherment of Maya hieroglyphic writing—the breaking of its "code"—is long and winding, marked by misleading theories, personal rivalries, and false Rosetta stones. But, in the end, the tale is a triumph of international scholarly collaboration.

As of 1800 CE, explorers had drawn, but not published, a mere handful of glyphs. By 1900, they had identified the Long Count calendar and correlated it with the Western calendar, but half a century later, noncalendric glyphic texts still could not be read. Misleading theories hindered progress. Maya glyphs were not simply Egyptian-style logograms. Nor were they limited to information on the cosmos. The Maya "alphabet" written down by Diego de Landa in sixteenth-century Yucatan, complete with glyphs corresponding to Spanish letters, was based on the Franciscan friar's misunderstanding of Maya writing; it was not the key to the code that many assumed it to be.

In the 1950s, however, breakthroughs by epigraphers in Europe, Mexico, and the United States combined to lay the foundation for increasingly rapid progress in subsequent decades. Three discoveries proved crucial: the heavy phonetic and syllabic component to Maya script, the ubiquity of emblem glyphs or place names, and the historical patterning of inscriptions. In other words, Mayanists realized that glyphs recorded the spoken word, telling the histories of real people, where and when they lived, who their ancestors were, with whom they fought, and how they conceived their connections to the past, to the natural world, and to the cosmos. Since the 1980s, epigraphers have used increasingly sophisticated linguistic methodologies, combining them with iconographic analysis, to reconstruct the detailed histories of Maya individuals, the objects and buildings they created, the cities in which they lived, and—perhaps most astonishing—the ideas that guided them.

other literary possibilities. But that complexity outfoxed early generations of Mayanists, and scholars in the early twenty-first century continue to discover new meanings in the ever-growing corpus of deciphered glyphic texts.

The second question prompted by the story of the decipherment of Maya writing is, What did the Maya write about? In what way did the glyphs' textual content change our understanding of the Maya past? Most surviving glyphic texts recorded the history of Classic-era kingdoms and the glories of their ruling dynasties. Indeed, much of what we know about the Maya from the third century BCE through the sixteenth century CE comes from records in hieroglyphs. Only by reading those texts are we able to recover the names, occupations, and life experiences of individual Mayas and the deep histories of their hometowns.

In the Early Classic centuries, Mayas simultaneously developed and expanded the surfaces on which they could write and the sophistication of the writing system itself. Some Mayanists like to think of these two things as metaphorical hardware and software. The hardware grew in terms of concept, scale, and variety. Monuments, stairways, and walls were designed to incorporate larger and more complex texts, almost always combined with sculpture. Ceramics evolved from the Early Classic's low bowls with small surfaces for writing to tall, upright tripod vessels offering larger surfaces (and separate lids) for script; they then evolved into the Classic period's ubiquitous tall cylinder—as much a medium for narrative text and art, if not more so, than a container for food, drink, or valued heirloom objects.

At the same time—through a dynamic relationship between the two—the "software" evolved from being equally logographic and phonetic to being mostly phonetic. As scholars find and study inscriptions dated earlier and earlier, they date the origins of phonetic writing and the Maya glyphic syllabary earlier. That said, highly logographic script was suitable for the short notations of the centuries before the Early Classic period. Then, by the first centuries CE—and certainly by the fifth—the development and wider use of more sophisticated phonetic spellings, along with the creation of a complete syllabary, permitted the writing on ceramic, stone, and other "hardware" of more expansive texts. These allowed the writer to build narratives that moved backward and forward in time, that included lateral statements on the activities of the gods or the achievements of dynastic members or the events of intercity rivalries, and that were capable of conveying nuances such as ambiguity and implication. In other words, all the details that underpin the modern reconstruction of the world of the Classic Maya divine kings were made possible by these parallel hardware and software developments.

An example of this is the stela portrait of Lady K'abel (Figure 7). While the body of the queen takes up the majority of the composition, this figurative imagery is placed in close spatial relation to the hieroglyphic texts, which is intended to respond to the sculpture's iconographic codes. On the front and two sides of the sculpture, artists provided viewers with ninety-seven hieroglyphic blocks. The monument was clearly erected as a commemorative marker. The glyphs on Stela 34's two sides record lunar cycle information, a singular event in the Maya Long Count, and an additional date. On the front of the image, glyphs are scattered throughout the composition at various scales and depths of relief. These texts name the people portrayed, Lady K'abel and her dwarf, Pat Tuun Ahk. The smaller glyphs name the artists who designed and carved the monuments, these inscriptions being among only a few such artist signatures in the Maya world. The text block located at the top left of the composition is composed of a series of dates using multiple calendrical cycles, ending with the dedication of the monument in 692 CE.

Although tens of thousands of Maya inscriptions on stone and ceramic objects have survived, along with hundreds on media such as wood, shell, and bone, countless thousands of books perished. The Maya made paper (called *hu'un*) from beaten fig bark, smoothed with lime stucco and fashioned into strips typically nine inches high; those strips were painted with glyphs and images and then folded accordion style into books—called codices by Mayanists—about four inches wide. Reeds and quills were used as pens, and soot was turned into black ink.

Despite the ravages of a tropical climate, combined with the Spanish commitment to destroy texts they could not read (and assumed were all religious in content), we know what Maya codices were like for three reasons. First, the organic remnants of perhaps a dozen codices have been found in tombs by archaeologists. Second, painted ceramic vases depict books being written, read, and sometimes bound in jaguar-skin covers. Third, four codices have survived to this day, all created in the Late Postclassic or contact centuries. Three were spared priests' bonfires in Yucatan in the late sixteenth or early seventeenth centuries and sent to Europe (named the Dresden, Paris, and Madrid codices after the cities where they ended up; the thirty-nine-page Dresden is the most beautiful and complex). A fourth, the Grolier, was found in the 1960s by looters. These four codices use a more simplified and primarily phonetic variant on Classic-era hieroglyphs, and they are all devoted to calendrical and ritual matters, primarily eclipses and the astronomical cycles of Venus. Codices on other topics—ranging from historical to medicinal—must have existed, but did not survive, although some were copied in the colonial centuries into alphabetic books, such as the *Popol Vuh* in K'iche' and the *Books of Chilam Balam* in Yucatec.

Small-scale art

The Maya also excelled in artistic production at smaller scales. Examples have survived from commoner domestic contexts and from elite ones. Ceramics and the lapidary arts are the best represented in the archaeological record, although wooden carvings have also been found in architectural contexts, in caves, and at the watery bottom of *cenotes* (the natural pits or sinkholes found across the Yucatan Peninsula, caused by collapsed limestone bedrock). Carvings were likely thrown into *cenote* groundwater as sacrificial offerings. However, illustrated ceramics detail an entire world of more fragile objects composed of perishable materials such as textiles, paper, and feathers (as in the details of Figures 6–8).

Of all these media, jadeite appears to hold a particular importance for the ancient Maya, who believed it was a material imbued with soul or spirit. This explains its abundant presence in elite funerary contexts, where it was used for funerary masks and where a jade bead was frequently placed in the mouth of the deceased. It was also used for elaborately carved ritual paraphernalia, costume elements that housed representations of deities associated with known spiritual power. Evidence from excavated burials reveals that royalty and nobles sometimes wore small jadeite pendants, representing, for example, a Maya *ajaw* donning a headdress in the shape of a supernatural deity. Such objects are vibrant green, a color of sacred meaning for the ancient Maya, evoking life necessities such as running water and young corn. It is clear that jadeite pieces were frequently treated as heirloom pieces, handed down to Maya family members for generations or given to foreign dignitaries as objects of diplomatic exchange. Since most jadeite was mined and then traded from the Motagua River valley in contemporary Guatemala, the southern area of the Maya world, it was inherently an exotic resource and thus associated with foreign knowledge and expertise. Anyone wearing paraphernalia carved from this precious stone similarly embodied these attributes.

Ceramic vessels permeated every level of Maya society because they fulfilled both utilitarian and ceremonial functions. In both commoner and elite domestic contexts, rather simple forms were used for the daily tasks of food preparation, but for special occasions, all classes of Maya society had fancier serving wares. The royal courts undoubtedly owned the finest examples from this genre of artistic production, with exceptionally well-crafted and painted wares produced by known and sometimes named artists. In fact, some ceramic artists were so well known that their vessels were prized as gifts during moments of diplomatic exchange.

Now preserved in many museums are examples of a particular type of ceramic vessel, a tall, thin cylinder, usually used for the consumption of a cacao beverage that Maya rulers and nobles enjoyed (Figures 6 and 8). *Cacao* is derived from the Mayan *kakawa*, and the Maya were the first to develop the process of fermenting, drying, and roasting the seeds of the cacao tree to make drinkable chocolate. Maya chocolate jars or pots typically display vibrant moments of palace life, deities, war scenes, or elaborate abstract decoration rendered in vivid colors from a palette dominated by reds, browns, black, and yellow. These scenes are so complex and detailed that scholars are able to use them as windows onto Maya culture because they seem to function as snapshots of Maya life. In addition to their practical function as drinking cups, these vessels also had a political function, with certain designs chosen for public display during specific ceremonial and governmental moments. Because the drinking of chocolate was a privilege reserved for the high ranking, a sumptuary social divider as early as the first millennium BCE, cacao products and their ceramic vessels resonated deeply in Maya culture.

Artists modeled sculptures in clay in three dimensions, usually representing deities and, more infrequently, human actors. Archaeologists have uncovered thousands of effigy figures in home remains; they were in all Maya households, it seems. They are often diminutive, only measuring a few inches in height, but are detailed enough for scholars to determine exactly which supernatural being they are meant to represent. In elite contexts they can be more substantial, requiring firing in separate pieces that were assembled once the component parts were completed. Many of them at various scales contain a cavity within the body of the piece that allowed for them to serve as stylized incense burners; in some cases, residue analysis revealed that the Maya burned a local tree resin, copal (*pom*), inside them, presumably during religious and other rituals.

Similarly, Maya artists crafted clay to represent the diverse human types of the Maya world. An island off the west coast of the Yucatan Peninsula, Jaina, was used since the Preclassic period as a graveyard of sorts. Thousands of Mayas were interred with small-scale figurines: musicians, women weaving and caring for children, embracing couples, and costumed ballplayers, all rendered with exquisite attention and vibrantly painted. Other sites scattered throughout the Maya area have also revealed figurines similar to those from Jaina. It is still debated whether these are true portraits. More likely they do not depict actual historical actors, but rather mere "types" of Maya peoples. That said, a distinct class of these objects certainly represented historical *ajawtaak* (rulers), many of which were excavated from commoner contexts (as in Motul de San José, for example).

The built environment

The most basic Maya structure is rectilinear or ovoid, with walls composed of wattle and daub (a combination of pole uprights and mud), topped with a peaked, thatched roof. These were (and in some places still are) the homes of Maya farmers, frequently arranged around an open patio. Historically, Mayas lived in patrilocal, extended kin groups. Upon their death, family members were commonly interred in the house floors, fusing the domestic spaces of the living and their deceased (sometimes deified) ancestors.

While the Classic Maya (and Mesoamerican societies in general) are best known for their monumental stepped pyramids, their architectural accomplishments represent a more varied structural suite. The typical urban design of the Late Classic period,

9. A fine example of Maya architectural splendor is Tikal's Great Plaza, featuring Temple I (on the left), Temple II (on the right), and the royal palace (in the background on the far side of the plaza).

featuring towering structures clustered around open paved plazas, is exemplified by the metropolis of Tikal, redesigned after a century-long hiatus by *ajaw* Jasaw Chan K'awiil I. His greatest architectural achievement was a complete reorientation of the city's central core. Jasaw Chan K'awiil I oversaw the creation of a new palace complex, with two inward-facing monumental stepped pyramids, all the while maintaining the structural and design integrity of his ancestors' necropolis, used for elite burials for centuries. The result was the "Great Plaza" (as Mayanists call it), a bilaterally symmetrical urban center that visually and spatially consolidated the political and religious power of the *ajaw* by bringing the architectural symbols of the dead, the living, ritual, and politics into a single structural complex, perhaps echoing the traditions of household architecture.

The conflation of these human realms is perhaps best demonstrated by Jasaw Chan K'awiil I's funerary monument, the monumental Temple I, which borders the eastern side of the plaza. Presumably designed by the ruler before his death, it was certainly completed by his son, who succeeded his father to the throne. Temple I is composed of nine superimposed terraces, a reference to the nine levels of Xibalba, through which Maya rulers must pass before being reborn as deified entities. It is topped with the paradigmatic temple, house sized and house shaped. A close, claustrophobic space, architects intended these inner sanctums to replicate the spatial experience of naturally occurring caves, conceived of as portals to the Underworld and thus ideal locations to commune with deities and deified ancestors. A vaulted tomb was discovered deep within the matrix of Temple I, containing the body and elaborate grave goods of Jasaw Chan K'awiil I. This tomb resides beneath the plaza floor, signaling that the temple was completed after the ruler's death in 734.

The spatial closeness of Temple I's upper sanctuary and its interior tomb came from desired architectural features that also stemmed from the nature of Maya building technology. Maya buildings relied on the enclosure of interior space by way of the corbeled vault or arch; the true arch, as developed by the ancient Romans, was never used in precontact Mesoamerica. A technology based on the gradual placing of rectilinear stones closer and closer together in a vertical alignment, the corbel arch is not inherently stable, necessitating the use of heavy fill on top of the arch to hold the component stones in place. This makes Maya buildings extremely top heavy and likely to collapse given the passage of time and intervention of tree roots and heavy rain. It also limited the width of each building, causing Maya edifices to feel restrictive. Architects in Late Classic Palenque developed a technique of "piggybacking" corbeled roof vaults by connecting them at right angles to increase the width of structures in that city.

Other Late Classic rulers advertised their political might via large-scale urban projects. Copan's 18-Rabbit oversaw the redesign of one of his city's central squares, called the Great Plaza (Figure 5). Here, he created a ritual space punctuated by several of his own portrait stelae. These monumental sculptures displayed the ruler in various states of ceremonial trance and were the stopping points in a sequence of ritual acts carried out over a *k'atun*, or twenty-year period. Thus, urban design and its component material together functioned as timekeeping devices that served to preserve, in permanent form, an *ajaw*'s control over time itself.

At Copan, this Great Plaza was separated from the rest of the urban core by a relatively small four-sided pyramid, with staircases on each side climbing to its summit. On its southern side rose the architectural bulk of Copan's center, dominated by the massive pyramid/mound complex of Temple 16, completed by the city's last Classic Period ruler, Yax Pasaj Chan Yopaat.

Although it is the tallest building at Copan, its grandeur has been overshadowed in intellectual circles by the edifice that lies cater-cornered to it, Structure 26. The founder of Copan's dynasty, K'inich Yax K'uk' Mo', originally built the temple in the mid-fifth century; the city's fifteenth ruler, K'ahk' Yipyaj Chan K'awiil, completed the final remodeling. Its western façade features the famous Hieroglyphic Stairway, a processional staircase composed of sixty-two steps made of 2,200 individual glyph blocks and punctuated by three-dimensional portraits of past *ajawtaak*. This is the longest hieroglyphic text yet found in the Maya world, providing scholars with a complete dynastic history of the city from the fifth century to the eighth.

Not surprisingly, monumental manifestations of Maya cultural achievements—such as the Tikal's Great Plaza and Copan's Hieroglyphic Stairway—have received the most attention from scholars and the interested public alike; it is indisputable that the civilizational developments of the Classic centuries were remarkable. However, they have tended to overshadow the more mundane aspects of Maya life, which are just as pertinent to defining their civilization.

Chapter 5
A day in the life

The most impressive hallmarks of Maya civilization—spectacular buildings in sprawling cities, intriguing glyphic texts accompanying stunning carvings and paintings—were created for thousands of years across the Maya region; such achievements will surely continue to capture our imagination for centuries to come. But that legacy of dazzling art and architecture created a distorted view of the ancient Maya, ever since archaeologists and other scholars began to reconstruct their past. To some extent, the distortions stem from the emphasis—both popular and scholarly—on the Maya as mysterious. But they also stem from the emphasis on elite life—on the dynastic and noble families who lived in and among the great stone buildings and who were immortalized by the art they commissioned or created. To reach a more balanced view of the Maya world, we must consider those aspects of daily life that a nonelite Maya family might have experienced.

The cycle of family life

Nonelite Maya homes were simple structures, usually comprising a single room. But that does not mean that Maya family life was confined or nuclear. On the contrary, no Mayan language had a term that corresponds closely to our "family." Instead, kinship was defined more broadly to include multiple generations, lateral kin,

kin by marriage, and fictive kin. The layout of Maya homes reflected that concept of kinship ties; they were clustered around patios and small plazas—outdoor spaces that were used for family activities as much as indoor ones were. Plaza or courtyard groups of multiple structures were often grouped into larger residential clusters, which we might call lineage neighborhoods.

Maya children thus grew up as much among cousins as among siblings and as much with grandparents and their siblings as with parents. At the onset of puberty, boys and girls underwent various rituals and rites of passage—one of which was a blessing ceremony that sixteenth-century Spanish friars imagined was a kind of Maya "baptism." After these rituals, girls remained at home but were eligible for marriage, whereas boys were removed from their homes—at least for part of the time and according to colonial evidence—to be trained in the arts of warfare, hunting, trading, the ball game, or other skills for which they seemed suited. Young Maya men were not marginalized by adult life, but were a focal point of attention. That attention was sometimes loving, sometimes anxious, but above all, they celebrated adolescence as the glorious passage to manhood.

As was the case elsewhere in Mesoamerica (and, indeed, worldwide), gender roles included a double standard of sexual and marital practice. Girls were raised strictly and chastely, suffering severe punishment for promiscuity, and they were obliged to marry according to arrangements made by parents and lineage elders. In Postclassic and colonial Yucatan, it was taboo to marry within one's *chibal* (patronym group or patrilineage), so marriages bound lineages together, a practice that likely extended back in time and across the Maya area. Boys and men, however, enjoyed more freedom; although adultery was banned (colonial sources claimed it was punishable by death), men could visit prostitutes and acquire as many wives as they could afford—with polygamy a marker of elite status.

Maya personal identity was marked by patronym, or the *chibal* surname of one's father. In Yucatan, there were some 250 patrilineages in the sixteenth century, and their names carried sufficient social significance to survive the cultural changes of the colonial and modern periods. They are still in use in the early twenty-first century. Mayas also inherited names from their mothers, with matrilineal descent therefore important (albeit less so), apparently playing a role in marriage arrangements and in gender-based economic activities. For example, women wove cloth and did other work in and around the home, and they tended to pass on to their daughters property inherited from their mothers. The higher ranked a person was, the more emphasis was placed on their paternal and maternal descent, because lineage conveyed social rank and gave access to land and wealth. For members of royal or elite dynastic lineages, descent was everything; it could even link a person to the gods.

At the other end of the social scale, the poorest commoners were known less by their ancestry and more by their calendrical names (determined by day of birth), childhood nicknames, or occupational labels. The same would have been true of most slaves because it appears that the most common avenue into slavery was to be a commoner captured in battle—elite warriors were kept as hostages or ritually executed—or to be the child of such a captive. Colonial-era sources also claim that in earlier centuries criminals were condemned to slavery. Either way, there is no evidence of a slave trade or of extensive slavery in the Maya world before Spaniards arrived in the sixteenth century and introduced into the area a trade in enslaved Africans, Mayas, and other indigenous peoples.

Death returned Maya men and women to where they had come from, not just to their lineage neighborhoods but also to the cluster of houses where they grew up—even to the home in which they were born, beneath whose floor they were buried. Commoner burials were conceptually the same as elite ones, only by definition of social status far more modest. The commoner's equivalent to the splendid royal tomb, sealed beneath a towering pyramidal temple and filled with the sacred wealth of treasure, was to be interred with a jade bead in the mouth, along with a few material goods that the deceased treasured in life. Such items might include small, carved statues (what Europeans would later call *idols*), beads, or a ceramic vessel (perhaps with the owner's name on it). Colonial sources claim that scribes and priests were buried with hieroglyphic books. Archaeologists have found that in some cities the dead were cremated or their heads were mummified (as in Postclassic Mayapan), but such practices seem to have been restricted to the elite.

Food and forests

The Maya area is environmentally challenging for humans. With its riverless scrub forest to the north, its tropical rainforest in the middle, and its volcanic mountain ranges in the south, it is an unlikely place for a civilization to develop—let alone one so complex and persistent. Yet not only were there millions of Mayas at peak population points (perhaps as many as 10 million), but also Maya farmers produced sufficient food to support a sizeable minority of people who built, carved, painted, crafted, weaved, traded, fought, ruled, and spent their days in many other activities that did not directly feed families. How was that possible?

The key to Maya civilization was either achievement in agriculture or skill at adapting to the rainforest—depending on which Mayanist one believes. Regardless of whether the focus is on crop farming or the forest garden, on beekeeping and fruit tree cultivation or on the hunting and domestication of animals, the goal for Mayanists is to understand how the Maya developed such successful technologies and cultures of food production and distribution—almost entirely at local or regional levels, without area-wide imperial authorities to direct the process. That does not mean that the Maya relationship with their environment was flawless. On the contrary, periods of ecological crisis or environmental catastrophe were not only the result of natural occurrences such as prolonged drought, insect plagues, hurricanes, earthquakes, floods, and volcanic eruptions; they were also prompted by overfarming, overpopulation, and the disruptions of warfare. But the failures of the system were the exceptions that reveal how well it served millions of Mayas for many centuries.

Maize was the Maya staple, so fundamental to the diet that it enjoyed a mythological, sacred reverence; it is probably fair to say that most Maya men were corn farmers, and they believed that maize was a divine gift. Maize domestication was first achieved in southern Mexico and the Maya area. Mayas were growing corn by at least 4,000 years ago. Many scholars believe that the manipulation of maize genetics to create larger corn cobs and higher-yielding races of maize and improvements in how maize was prepared—the advent of that *nixtamal* process—made the Preclassic transition to larger, denser settlements and the genesis of Maya cities possible.

Certainly by Preclassic times, corn was being cultivated throughout the Maya area, supplemented by beans, squash, chili peppers, root crops, and fruits. Salt was as crucial as corn, acquired through salt boiling in regions like southern Belize or—more commonly—through the trade networks that brought it from the massive salt beds of Yucatan's north coast lagoons. Because the Yucatan Peninsula is flat and virtually riverless, its people favored sites with *cenotes* for town building, and farmers created wells, canals, and reservoirs. Foods and other products from outside Yucatan could also be exchanged for the peninsula's trade or "cash" crops—primarily cotton, which has a deep history of cultivation in the region, but also beeswax, honey, and cacao (although cacao groves were more common to the south, in Tabasco, Belize, and Guatemala's Pacific coast).

In the rainforest, the Maya seem to have understood that it was crucial to mimic and maintain the natural diversity and dispersion of edible fruits and crops. In other words, by avoiding overcollecting, overfarming, excessive clearing, or monocultivation, the Maya found that the numerous ecological niches and levels of the rainforest could provide a steady and varied diet. Farmers kept rainforests mostly intact; even at Tikal, whose population peak may have been several hundred thousand, forest removal never exceeded 60 percent. Furthermore, when clearing was carried out in forests, the culling was highly selective (a fruit tree, for example, would never be cut down), gradually creating a curated forest in and around settlements (an artificial rainforest, some have called it). Whereas access was the primary water challenge in Yucatan, in rainforest regions water control was more important—and Maya engineers achieved it through the increasingly sophisticated use (from Preclassic to Postclassic eras) of raised fields, terracing, and hydraulic engineering.

Although it might be anachronistic to think of the Maya as environmentalists, their ecological attitudes tended to balance innovation and exploitation with restraint or respect for the environment. That was as true for agriculture as it was for animal husbandry and hunting. Dogs were domesticated: some breeds for eating, others for use in the hunt. Turkeys were both hunted in the wild and bred at home. Apiculture also has deep roots in Maya civilization; the native stingless bee was raised across the Maya area, but especially in Yucatan. Deer and peccary (a local javelina or skunk pig) were hunted, as was the armadillo and a wide variety of fowl. Lagoon, river, and coastal fishing were extensive; there were even commercial fisheries on the Caribbean coast. The enormous diversity of rainforest fauna included jaguars, ocelots, deer, fox, rabbits, agoutis, tapirs, and boar—all used by Mayas for food, pelts, tools, and ornaments.

These animals, along with monkeys and numerous tropical birds, were elemental not just to the Maya diet, but also to the daily experience of wildlife and the fundamental way in which Mayas viewed life in their world. Within their own neighborhoods and cities, each Maya's link to animals and birds reflected his or her social status. For example, while it may be obvious that wearing feathers from the rare and spectacular quetzal bird marked a Maya as noble or royal, scholars have also analyzed strontium isotope levels in bones and teeth to show that elites ate more deer—and better cuts of it—than lower-ranked Mayas. Wildlife also linked Mayas to the past and to the supernatural realm because the mythology that underpinned understandings of human origins and of the deities was filled with monkeys, birds, serpents, and other creatures.

Mayanists used to wonder how the relatively small kingdoms of the Maya area could sustain dense populations with limited resources. But, in light of the numerous archaeological discoveries of the many ways in which the ancient Maya flourished in diverse environments, Mayanists have now upended the question of how royal rulers could feed their subjects without the sweeping power of empire. As it turns out, ecological adaptation succeeded *because* it was decentralized and localized in its conception and control. By sharing a common culture but not a single political system, Mayas may have enjoyed the best of both worlds. Through trade and migration, foodstuffs and ideas on how to best produce them spread from region to region. But when city-states tried to create hegemonies or small empires—as Tikal, Calakmul, and Caracol did in the Classic centuries—they eventually failed, going down in history as exceptions that proved the rule that a plurality of Maya polities prospered because they reflected environmental diversity.

A day in the life

Going downtown

The pendulum of scholarly opinion on the nature of Maya urbanism has swung back and forth since the early twentieth century. Some Mayanists once envisioned Maya cities as mere ceremonial centers with restricted access—making them not really

63

cities at all and the Maya a nonurban civilization. Others have imagined places like Classic Tikal or Postclassic Mayapan as bustling hives of political, social, and economic activity, with a daily migration into the center by workers and traders from outlying settlements that resonates with our modern understanding of city and suburb, center and satellite.

Reality for much of Maya history was likely a combination of those two models, but closer to the latter. The network of elevated plazas that comprised city centers was often designed to be easily closed off, sometimes for defensive purposes but often to control spaces where ruling lineages resided, granting access to nonelite subjects under specific circumstances. But there were many such circumstances, many reasons for an "ordinary" Maya man or woman to be—or to go—downtown. Furthermore, city centers were linked to lineage neighborhoods and to adjacent towns with the straight, raised, plastered causeways called *sacbeob*. It was not boundary walls or streets that defined neighborhoods, but focal nodes, such as water sources or small neighborhood temples, plazas, and ball courts. Socially, lineage and craft specialization defined neighborhoods. But neighborhoods were not necessarily homogeneous. Maya cities were often more like modern cities than previously thought, with population densities up to 3,000 people per square kilometer and considerable wealth differences within neighborhoods as much as between them.

Maya cities were webs of causeways and paths. At the mundane or daily level, domestic servants or slaves walked into the center from their own residential neighborhoods to work for their masters. Skilled laborers enlarging pyramidal mounds and palaces or decorating their elaborate façades made similar daily journeys. At weekly or monthly intervals, traders carried in the wares to participate in markets, and buyers followed them; no Maya city or town was complete without a roofed marketplace facing one of its central plazas. Porters also came in with food or animals, and musicians brought their instruments for ritual, seasonal festivals—which drew large crowds from surrounding settlements or urban satellites, just as ball games did. Whether they went downtown as a daily routine or for seasonal events, Mayas saw familiar faces. But at the same time, many cities were large and dense enough for encounters with strangers, including unknown residents of the same city, to be unremarkable.

The abundant and monumental open plazas that grace every Maya city were surely arenas for public dances, poetry orations, and musical performances, as preludes or in parallel to ball games. Classic-era art depicts musicians parading in set sequences, with maraca players and singers followed by trumpeters, turtle-shell rattlers, and drummers. Royal courts no doubt had their own composers and orchestras. Their skill, like the athletic prowess of the ballplayers who could bounce rubber balls off their hips and through hoops, was relished and celebrated as much as by the common townspeople as by the elite who sponsored them.

On occasion, many of these activities—playing, trading, consuming, celebrating—came together at a political climax, inspired and connected to the great political and religious rituals of Maya kingdoms: the accession and coronation of a new *ajaw* or the return of victorious warriors with prisoners to be ritually displayed, humiliated, and executed. Such moments celebrated city-state identity and would have been highly memorable for nonelite Mayas—whether slaves, corn-farming men, weaving women, or the merchants, stonemasons, artist-scribes, ballplayers, warriors, and priests who occupied the middle levels of society.

Even on less momentous days, Classic-era cities were decorated with stone-carved and brightly colored records of past coronations and triumphs, accompanied by hieroglyphic texts. We cannot know exactly how Maya commoners responded to royal performances in plazas; perhaps they enjoyed them without necessarily accepting the ideologies that such performances communicated. Nonetheless, they surely felt invested in their city

The Maya ball game

A defining cultural practice among the Maya, and among Mesoamericans in general, is a sporting event known to us as the "Mesoamerican ball game"; the Maya may have called the game *pitz*. We cannot know exactly what it was like to experience a game of *pitz*, either as player or as spectator, and the exact rules remain elusive (and likely varied through time and between regions), but players clearly competed to send balls through vertical carved-stone hoops, without using their hands or feet. Architectural evidence makes the sport's cultural, political, and religious importance obvious; numerous monumental ball courts graced the ceremonial centers and southern edges of most major cities. They were built in various formats, but the majority are composed of a long, rectilinear playing field bounded on the short ends by either one end zone (T-shaped ball court) or two (I-shaped ball court). The courts were separated from elevated pyramids by open plazas, which architects designed with seating for viewing the game, often with auxiliary temples. Stone carvers decorated stone side walls, hoops, and markers with pictorial reliefs. In Copan, the ball court sits in the city's very center, separating the acropolis from the Great Plaza designed by 18-Rabbit.

Not all ball courts were so splendid, however. Mayas practiced the sport at all levels of the social hierarchy, from humble "sandlot" pickup games in modest neighborhood courts to elaborate interregional competitions. The sport figured prominently in the mythistory of the *Popol Vuh*, whereby the Hero Twins were forced to play ball against the Lords of the Underworld. As such, the game likely had religious significance, with games perhaps being understood as re-enactments of this supernatural battle. Like modern sports, the Maya ball game was more a celebration of community, teamwork, and individual prowess than the blood sport of popular perception, outdated guidebooks, and bad movies.

and its well-being through their labor and their local lineage identities; ancestor-built, temple pyramids were landmarks that inspired civic pride.

We also cannot be certain of literacy rates in Maya communities. But it is likely that while only the elite minority was fully literate, many Mayas could read basic glyphs and identify dates and the names of hometowns and local rulers. Thus, even on the most ordinary downtown daytrip, nonelite Mayas were exposed to the rich history, artistic traditions, architectural splendor, and cultural complexity that they inherited from their ancestors.

Chapter 6
Conquests

When the Spaniards landed on the coasts of the peninsula, beginning in 1517, an "emperor of this kingdom of Yucatan, named Tutul Xiu, who always resided in the heights of Mani [ruled] the Indians." This was according to Francisco de Cárdenas y Valencia, a parish priest in Yucatan who wrote a short history of the province in 1643. After a series of failed invasions in the 1520s and 1530s, Spaniards founded a new colony centered on Tiho—which they renamed after the Spanish city of Merida. According to Cárdenas y Valencia, that foundational moment in 1542 was made possible by the Emperor Tutul Xiu's "desire to see and know the bearded sons of the sun" (as they called Spaniards in "their books of paganisms and prophecies"). The priest claimed that, just as Moctezuma, the emperor of the Aztecs, had a quarter century earlier anticipated the return of the bearded lords, so this Maya "emperor" was keen to see ancient predictions fulfilled, to offer "much veneration and respect" to the Spaniards, and to "become a Christian."

Cárdenas y Valencia was wrong, of course. Both in spirit and in almost every detail, his account was a wildly inaccurate folk fantasy. But Spaniards believed it for generations (and, eventually, centuries) as a justification for invasion, conversion, and colonization. Tutul Xiu, like Moctezuma, viewed the conquistadors not as anticipated lords to be obeyed but as invaders to be handled and—eventually and reluctantly—accommodated. Tutul Xiu did reside in the town of Mani as a supreme ruler, a *halach uinic* ("True Man"). But he ruled a small regional kingdom—one of perhaps eighteen that covered the peninsula when Spanish invasions ended the Postclassic era. There was no peninsula-wide Maya Empire when Europeans first arrived; there had never been one.

But Maya city-states had previously experienced empire and the violent expansionism that is intrinsic to it. To the north of the Maya area, the fertile valleys of central Mexico had for many centuries witnessed the rise and fall of empires. At least two of those empires—one centered on Teotihuacan, another centered on Tula—had sent envoys (if not, as some have argued, invasion forces) and established outposts of some kind in the Maya world.

Around the turn of the sixteenth century, the most recent such empire—centered on Tenochtitlan, the city-state of the Mexica and known to us as the Aztec Empire—established outposts on the northwest Maya frontier. An Aztec invasion would surely have taken place, probably on Moctezuma's watch, were it not for the fact that in 1519 the Aztec Empire was itself invaded by another empire—that of the Spaniards.

Yet the ensuing Spanish–Aztec war did not spare the Maya from invasion. On the contrary, following the implosion of the Aztec Empire in 1521, Spaniards spent two and a half decades using extreme violence, mass enslavement, and hundreds of thousands of indigenous Mesoamerican warriors to gradually take over and expand that empire. Maya regions experienced a series of invasions from the 1520s to the 1540s. Only where large numbers of former Aztecs and other Mesoamericans accompanied Spanish conquistadors did invasion campaigns result in the foundation of permanent colonies. In a certain sense, then, an Aztec invasion did take place.

Still, the invasions of the sixteenth century, whether seen more traditionally as conquests by Spanish colonists or as more complex Spanish–Aztec or Spanish–Mesoamerican incursions, were protracted and incomplete. As with encounters centuries before with warriors and colonists from Teotihuacan, the Maya world was not and could not be overrun, conquered, and controlled—not in its entirety or even anything close to it.

The Terminal Classic and Postclassic eras

Three of the best known and most visited Maya sites in northern Yucatan are Uxmal in the west, Coba in the east, and, between them, Chichén Itzá. While the central Maya regions and their great cities were undergoing the transitions of the Terminal Classic (the so-called Collapse), this trio of Yucatec city-states expanded politically and flourished culturally.

From the eighth to eleventh centuries, all the towns in the peninsula's northern half at some point probably fell under the control of one or other of these three competing city-states. Systems of rule and mechanisms of expansion were rooted in Classic antecedents: *k'uhul ajawob* reigned over Uxmal, for example, at least through the tenth century, as evidenced by monuments glorifying divine kings like Lord Chaak. Where the continually shifting frontiers of influence between the three city-states met, satellite centers and border sites became fortified—an echo of earlier warfare patterns from regions to the south.

But Mayas also developed variants on their civilization's art and architecture. For example, the architectural style of Uxmal and the other Puuc cites—with their great arches, multistory palaces, and striking stone mosaic façades—was distinct from that of all other Maya regions. Differences in visual culture reflected divergent cultural practices. The polytheism of the Classic Maya persisted, but art in Yucatan now favored the representation of deities over political leaders, possible evidence of a slightly altered political system of the Classic period. For example, the role of a council of lineage heads seems to have tempered the authoritarianism of the *k'uhul ajaw* system. For most of Yucatan's Postclassic, the *ajaw* was no longer *k'uhul*, or divine, but merely dominant over the ruling council (*multepal*, "group of heads"). The councilors gathered not with heads bowed in a throne room, but circled in a *popolna*, or "mat house." Such evidence is stronger for the later Postclassic centuries, but surely stretched back into the era when Uxmal, Chichén Itzá, and Coba competed for control over swathes of the peninsula, jostling for access to trade routes, subordinate towns, agricultural and tribute products, and refugees from the south.

Another notable variant on traditional practice was the expansion of the *sacbeob*: to link their capitals to outlying subject towns, defensive zones, and trade points, Chichén Itzá and Coba built many miles of great white-washed causeways, which archaeologists are still uncovering. Aerial landscape surveys using Lidar have shown that "white road" networks were more extensive than was realized before such technology was available. This is true of other regions as well—Preclassic and Classic Peten, certainly—but the prevalence in Postclassic Yucatan of both internal *sacbeob* (Chichén Itzá had at least thirty) and intercity ones is notable.

Chichén Itzá's distinct style of art and architecture has proved to be particularly confounding and controversial to Mayanists. The layout of part of the city's center—combined with such features as colonnaded halls and atlantean columns, stone skull racks (*tzompantli* in the central Mexican language of Nahuatl), feathered-serpent imagery, and carved warriors wearing Toltec-style headdresses, shields, armor, and weapons—revealed close parallels to Toltec military culture. The Toltec Empire rose to dominate central Mexico in the tenth century, its capital of Tula flourishing until its sacking around 1160. In the middle of this period, Chichén Itzá achieved a brief hegemony over much of northern Yucatan, eclipsing Uxmal and Coba during the first half of the eleventh century. How were these two developments related?

It was long assumed that the story was a simple one: The Toltecs invaded and conquered Yucatan, created a regional imperial capital at Chichén Itzá, and introduced new artistic styles and political practices. Such practices included the highly ritualized, public executions (so-called human sacrifices) closely associated with central Mexican empires, from the Toltecs to the Aztecs. Furthermore, Toltec folk history tells of the flight from Tula in 987 of a king named Quetzalcoatl ("Feathered Serpent" in Nahuatl), while Yucatec folk history recounts the arrival between 967 and 987 of an invading foreigner named K'uk'ulkan ("Feathered Serpent" in Yucatec Maya), who made Chichén Itzá his capital. As tempting as that tale is, both those folk histories date from the colonial period, when indigenous traditions within Mesoamerican regions became influenced by each other and by Spanish and Christian cultures. Nonetheless, the K'uk'ulkan legend was surely part of a far more complex history of Tula–Chichén contact, perhaps similar to the earlier Teotihuacan–Tikal relationship.

For decades scholars believed that the architectural and iconographic similarities between central Mexico and Chichén Itzá during the Terminal Classic could only be evidence of the forceful takeover of the Yucatecan city by more powerful Toltec forces. But most Mayanists now believe that for most of its duration, the link was likely the result of sustained economic contact between the two regional empires—not the result of a Toltec conquest. It is possible this kind of contact was eventually cemented through dynastic marriages and other forms of diplomatic exchange that manifested in the development of a unique style of art and architecture that glorified the political regime—a concept that was fundamentally Maya, even if it looked strikingly Toltec.

Just as Tula was sacked, so was Chichén Itzá. Once believed to be the doing of the Itza—hence the city's subsequent name—it is now thought that the Itza dynasty ruled the city during its heyday and that other lineages overthrew the Itza. Forced to flee, the Itza leadership and their allies migrated south, establishing a small kingdom near Tikal (it was still called Itza or Peten Itza, "the Province of the Itza," when Spaniards finally invaded and destroyed it in 1697).

Meanwhile, after a period of political fragmentation, much of northern Yucatan again fell under the control of a single city-state, Mayapan. It may have been founded, or refounded, by an Itza lord named K'uk'ulkan, or that may be a foundational myth designed to legitimize Mayapan's control. Either way, by 1283 the Cocom lineage dominated a *multepal* style of government. Without the authoritarian direction of a *k'uhul ajaw*, Mayapan's center was composed only of simplified versions of the more monumental pyramids and palaces that graced neighboring Chichén Itzá. Over time, Mayapan developed into a substantial walled city of more than 2,000 buildings housing some 10,000 to 15,000 residents. Most of those inhabitants were from Mayapan or the region around it, but analysis of skeletal remains suggests that a minority came from throughout northern Yucatan (none from outside the Maya area).

Not until the middle of the fifteenth century did lineage rivalries break out into civil conflict and cause the collapse of Mayapan's regional supremacy. The Mani-based Xiu lineage deposed the Cocom in a political coup that seems to have been marked by a massacre of Cocom family members. But the Xiu were unable to displace the Cocom completely or to control the region that had been centered on Mayapan. Instead, an archipelago pattern of small kingdoms returned to the peninsula. Among those kingdoms, the Xiu controlled a wealthy one and the Cocom a smaller one, their rivalry still being played out a century later—parallel to, and part of, the history of the protracted Spanish invasion.

During these same seven centuries—the ninth to sixteenth, or the Terminal Classic through the Postclassic periods—many other regions of the Maya world saw city-states wax and wane. The general pattern was the ongoing development of regional cultures within a persistent Maya civilization, marked by a combination of local variants and influence from outside (specifically, other Maya regions or central and southern Mexico). Two regions in particular are worth brief mention: the east coast (from today's Cancun to Belize) and the Guatemalan highlands.

A series of small kingdoms flourished all down Yucatan's eastern seaboard from at least the thirteenth century, including the island of Cozumel to the north and the great river valley cities of Belize (such as Lamanai). These polities may have benefitted from the peninsula-wide stability of the Mayapan hegemony. Yet after its dissolution in the mid-fifteenth century, small Yucatec sites like Tulum and Santa Rita, as well as the larger ones in Belize, were still flourishing when Spaniards arrived; some lasted even longer, into or through the seventeenth century. The Maya of these coastal or riverine kingdoms were not oceangoing, but they plied the rivers, lagoons, and sea routes up and down the coast—within the relative shelter provided by the 560-mile-long Mesoamerican Barrier Reef (running from Cancun to Honduras). Indeed, the first Mayas to make contact with Europeans may have been the two dozen in a great canoe laden with trade goods who, as they traveled south along the Belizean coast in 1502, came across the ships of Christopher Columbus's fourth voyage.

Artistic styles in these coastal Postclassic kingdoms are strikingly similar. The details suggest that, despite the absence of political centralization, all the east coast kingdoms participated in a common cult of religious veneration. For example, the mural paintings of religious temples share an artistic style unique to this region and time, defined by decreased naturalism in the renderings of human bodies and the abundant use of Maya Blue—a vibrant turquoise hue that is remarkably resilient in the tropical climate. Despite its regional distinctiveness, some scholars call this aesthetic the "International style" because it seems related to artistic innovations in central Mexico, particularly the codex artistry of the Mixteca–Puebla region. The nature of this influence is not yet fully understood, but it suggests cultural contact between these disparate zones of Mesoamerica. Thus, even on the eastern edge of their civilizational area, Mayas continued the centuries-old tradition of receiving—perhaps seeking—and absorbing political, economic, and cultural influence from Mexico.

That was also true of highland Guatemala, whose kingdoms lay closer to Mexico and its sequential empires. It remains unclear whether these city-states—the largest of which was that of the K'iche'—had direct contact with the Toltecs or indirect contact via Chichén Itzá. But the highland Maya kingdoms seem to have had economic and cultural, if not political, connections of some kind with Tula and Chichén Itzá during their heyday, just as they maintained diplomatic and trade relations with the Aztecs several centuries later.

The governmental system of the K'iche' and their neighbors was very similar to the *multepal* system that developed in Postclassic Yucatan: There was a K'iche' *ajaw* or king, but he shared power with a king-elect, and both kings recognized the role played by councilors representing lineages and the neighborhoods or subject towns that those lineages dominated. Following an age-old pattern, the K'iche' kingdom expanded in the fifteenth century to control much of the highlands, until the city-state of the Kaqchikel revolted and regained independence.

Thus, when Spaniards first learned of the highland kingdoms in 1521, the K'iche' was just the largest of half a dozen polities, including medium-sized kingdoms such as those of the Kaqchikel and Mam and smaller city-states such as that of the Tz'utujil. They all shared cultural traditions, common origins, and often common ancestors—but at the same time, they were divided by mountainous terrain, by differences in language, and by long-term political rivalries. Those facts would greatly complicate Spanish efforts to create a colony in the highlands.

The Maya–Spanish Thirty Years War

In 1521, the K'iche' kings and the neighboring rulers in the highlands learned quickly of the siege and capture of Tenochtitlan by Spanish-Nahua forces. They were, not surprisingly, keen to grasp the long-range implications of the power shift at the heart of the Aztec Empire—a shift from the Mexica to other Nahuas (the city-states of Tetzcoco and Tlaxcala) and to invading Spanish colonists. In response, they sent envoys to the city of Mexico-Tenochtitlan, which in turn prompted the dispatch by Hernán Cortés of the first Spanish-Nahua military company officially licensed to invade the Maya world.

Led by Pedro de Alvarado, the company comprised 300 Spaniards, over 6,000 former Aztecs and other Nahuas, and thousands of other Mesoamerican warriors and support personnel. Attacking the K'iche' kingdom in 1524, the company destroyed much of its capital city of Utatlán, capturing and burning alive the K'iche' king (*ah pop*) and king-elect (*ah pop qamahay*). After coercing K'iche' warriors into joining the invasion, the company ravaged the adjacent Kaqchikel towns and the tiny lakeside kingdom of the Tz'utujil. Alvarado established the Kaqchikel city of Iximché—renamed Santiago—as the new colonial capital and base from which to subdue the surrounding Maya region, and he wrote to his patron, Cortés, announcing his success. But had he succeeded?

In fact, he had not. Far from establishing a new colony and Christian kingdom, Alvarado's forces marauded one region after another, destroyed local political order, and terrorized Maya families. His efforts to pit the K'iche', Kaqchikel, Tz'utujil, and other Maya kingdoms against each other brought not "pacification" (the term conquistadors favored) but slaughter, enslavement, famine, disease, and starvation. Political instability—like the epidemics of smallpox and other Old World diseases that came with the invaders—spread even beyond the reach of the conquistadors.

Despite his claims, Pedro de Alvarado abandoned highland Guatemala in 1526, leaving it to his brother Jorge to return the following year with an even larger force of Nahua and other Mesoamerican warriors. The old Maya kingdoms, devastated by the first invasion, could not offer coordinated resistance. As a result, the second invasion enabled its leaders to establish a permanent Spanish-Nahua colony. But violence and sporadic warfare persisted into the 1540s, and the new colonial province comprised only a portion of the highlands and almost none of the central Maya area—with independent Maya polities stretching far to the north and into the Yucatan Peninsula. Even the tiny colony of La Vera Paz ("The True Peace")—located in the northern region of the highlands and founded not by conquistadors, but by Bartolomé de Las Casas and other Dominican friars in 1537—had collapsed by 1556. The good intentions of the friars could not withstand demands on Maya produce and labor by Spanish settlers, who classified Maya protest as "rebellion," using that in turn to justify violence and enslavement.

How Spaniards and Mayas experienced the wars of conquest in Guatemala was similar to how invaders and defenders experienced the Maya–Spanish Thirty Years War of 1517–47 throughout the Maya area. There were no quick conquests. Everywhere, protracted warfare was marked by repeated invasions. Spaniards could not establish colonies without using non-Spanish warriors, both allied Mayas and other Mesoamericans—most notably Nahuas (Figure 10)—and even then the colonies were relatively small. In most regions of the

Quauhtemallã.

Maya area, invasions failed; numerous small, independent polities survived outside and along an unstable colonial frontier.

The war's first year (1517) saw the first full-scale battle between conquistadors and a Maya army. It took place on the beaches of Yucatan and was recorded as a costly victory by the Spaniards, although it is clear to us—even with nothing but Spanish accounts as sources—that the encounter was a resounding military success for the Maya; a third of the Spanish company was killed, including their leader, and the survivors sailed right back to Cuba, instead of going on to discover the Aztec Empire.

The final year (1547) saw the final killings of the third major *entrada* or invasion campaign in Yucatan led by one or more of the three Franciscos de Montejo. The father, the *adelantado* (holder of a royal license to conquer and settle), led the first failed expedition in 1527, with his son, his nephew, Alonso Dávila, and a few other captains leading subsequent efforts. Symbolic of conquistador hubris was Ciudad Real ("Royal City"), a failed colonial capital that Spaniards founded in 1532 in the center of the largely abandoned Chichén Itzá. Had Montejo the Younger and his compatriots been right in believing they had won the full cooperation of the surrounding Maya kingdoms, today's archaeological site would not exist; it would have been razed and buried beneath a modern metropolis of over a million inhabitants (as Merida, built over the Maya city of Tiho, is in the early twenty-first century). But the Spaniards were deluded, and within months Maya leaders sprang their trap, chasing survivors out of the peninsula.

10. **In a Hispanocentric engraving (top) printed in 1595 as an illustration for a book that recounted the conquest of the Americas, the Flemish artist Theodor de Bry reimagined Maya warriors fighting foreign invaders (led by Spaniard Francisco de Montejo). A rare Nahuacentric view of the invasion of highland Guatemala (bottom) is found in a colonial-era painting on cloth by a Tlaxcalteca artist.**

Most conquest events occurred in the thirty years between 1517 and 1547, but not all: independent Maya kingdoms lasted into the seventeenth century, when the unconquered zone (Spaniards sometimes claimed it was *despoblado*, "uninhabited"), between the colony of Yucatan in the north and that of Guatemala in the highlands to the south, grew in size. Its largest kingdom, the polity of the Itza of the Peten, was not attacked and destroyed by Spanish forces until 1697. Even after that, independent Maya polities persisted, most notably in eastern Yucatan. They briefly threatened to take over the whole peninsula at the height of the Caste War in the 1840s, surviving into the next century; the final subjugation of an independent Maya polity by a Hispanic-led armed force was the attack on the village of Dzula in southeast Yucatan in 1933.

Clearly, then, it makes little sense to talk of "the Spanish conquest" of the Maya. The Maya were not conquered; rather, they developed various strategies of resistance and accommodation to outside invaders and influences, permitting a gradual evolution of their civilization over the past half millennium. Arguably, that pattern of response goes back even further and can be applied to Maya history since the Early Classic, if not before. But that prompts the question: Why, instead of a simple conquest in the sixteenth century, were there invasion wars that were so disparate and protracted (whether we count them as being 30, 180, or 400 years long)?

Early historians—Mexican and US scholars of the nineteenth and early twentieth centuries—had a pair of answers, both reflecting their Hispanocentric viewpoint. One was that Maya regions lacked gold and silver to tempt conquistadors, who were drawn to conquest campaigns in other regions. The other answer was rooted in the prejudicial perspective of the conquistadors themselves. One American historian denounced the Maya as "stubborn," blaming their "resistance" and "opposition" for making "the conquest [of the Maya] long drawn out, painful, and halting."

He echoed the complaints of conquistadors such as Cortés—that Mayas in the Peten and adjacent regions were "very bellicose and bold in war" and had thus "done much harm to the Spaniards" (1525)—and like those who founded Merida, lamenting the following year (1543) that "these Indians have forced us into many battles and denied us entry into their land, because they are indomitable Indians, a bellicose people."

By the seventeenth century, when Franciscans such as Cárdenas y Valencia and Diego López de Cogolludo were writing histories of the invasion wars, the Mayas had been turned into diabolistic cannibals. For example, Cogolludo claimed that two Spanish conquistadors seized by Maya warriors in the failing colony at Champoton in the late 1530s were promptly "sacrificed to their idols, and afterwards they ate them, as was their custom, keeping the small part [penis?] as a relic (according to an ancient account), the Devil thus not neglected, as on this occasion he surely incited their appetite for the taste of Spanish flesh."

Such explanations will not satisfy us. There is, in fact, no evidence that the Postclassic Maya were cannibals devoted to slaughtering captives in religious rituals, despite the popular (and sometimes scholarly) obsession with "human sacrifice"—vividly reflected in images stretching from early modern European woodcuts accompanying accounts of discovery and conquest to modern equivalents such as Mel Gibson's 2006 movie *Apocalypto*. There is no doubt that the Maya ritually executed war captives, people judged as criminals, and people, animals, plants, and objects chosen as religious offerings. But such executions have been practiced in almost all human cultures. Nor were all such rituals in Maya society necessarily religious, despite the Western tendency to exoticize and exaggerate Maya executions as always religious and always human sacrifice. Maya culture was no less violent than any other, but nor was it any more so. Thus, by viewing Maya–Spanish warfare from the perspective of Postclassic Maya political and military culture, we can explain the nature and outcome of the wars, while also maintaining our focus on Maya (not Spanish conquistador) history.

Because the Maya were never politically unified within an empire or culturally unified by a sense of common identity, there were as many as forty independent polities across the Maya area around 1500 CE. Mere short-term rivalries between ruling lineages divided some polities from others; deeper differences of language and community identity divided others. In the words of Gaspar Antonio Chi—who was born into the Xiu lineage in the middle of the Maya–Spanish wars and became the leading Maya–Spanish interpreter in sixteenth-century Yucatan—"when the conquistadors invaded these provinces, the provinces were already divided, and as each one was an enemy of the other, they fought with one another on little pretext, going out with their captains and their banners, most of them naked, painted with black stripes as a mark of future grief."

Conquistador captains sought to leverage regional rivalries and deploy one Maya polity against another (believing the oversimplified stories of how the Aztec and Inca Empires had been similarly subjugated). It worked only to a certain extent. In highland Guatemala, the Alvarado brothers benefited from the willingness of the K'iche', Kaqchikel, and Tz'utujil to use the disruption of the Spanish invasion to pursue old vendettas. The Montejo cousins and Alonso Dávila escaped with their lives after disastrous campaigns into eastern and southeastern Yucatan in the late 1520s and early 1530s because anti-Spanish cooperation between Maya polities was sporadic and because local leaders could not resist the temptation of sending the dangerous and demanding foreigners into neighboring kingdoms (wounded, exhausted, disoriented, and undernourished invaders were all too easily manipulated). And in the north, the willingness of Xiu, Cocom, and Pech leaders to pursue old rivalries between and during Spanish invasions helped the Montejos found Merida at Tiho in 1542, just as the persistent antipathy of those dynasties toward the northeast kingdoms helped the new colonial province survive into the next decade.

But more often than not, turning neighboring Maya polities against each other exacerbated traditional enmities, fostering regional warfare that postponed or prevented colonization. Thus, the Alvarados' stirring up of K'iche'–Kaqchikel rivalry contributed to two decades of brutal violence in the highlands—arguably, the region still struggles with this legacy. The result of the so-called Great Maya Revolt of 1546–47 (the final campaign into Yucatan's northeast, marking two decades of invasion violence in the region) was not to extend the frontier of the colonial province, but to help ensure there *was* a frontier for centuries to come. The failure of the Spanish Conquest in what is now southern Quintana Roo and Belize proved to be permanent.

The tactic of exploiting Maya political divisions suited strategies that were both short term and small in scale. Resulting colonies were destined to remain stunted (like Acalan and Higueras) or to grow painfully slowly (like highland Guatemala and northwest Yucatan). Nahuas and other indigenous central Mexicans were willing to travel long distances to fight and settle, as they had been doing for centuries. But Mayas lacked an equivalent imperial tradition, willing to fight only known neighbors rather than distant strangers. Tales of long-distance migration and conquest among the K'iche', Kaqchikel, Itza of the Peten, and Yucatec Maya were preserved at the level of mythologized community history rather than recent precedent. Not until the seventeenth century did Maya warriors engage in long-distance campaigns, as units of *indios flecheros* (indigenous archers) led by town *batabob* (Maya governors) in campaigns into the southern lowlands.

A further factor lies in the *multepal* style of Postclassic Maya governance. The authoritarian *ajawob* were long gone. It is not clear how much authority ruling councils enjoyed—and there were surely variants across the Maya area—but to some extent they offset the executive power of dynastic leaders who held varying titles and positions as co-kings, war captains, and religious officers. New arrangements and alliances would have required complex negotiations, easily prolonged or undone by mortality (in battle or from epidemic disease) or internal political or dynastic dissension.

One might expect such a system would produce differences of opinion in how to respond to outsiders, with initial interest leading to inconsistency, perhaps even alternating friendship and hostility; and that is precisely what Spanish captains complained about, interpreting the phenomenon in terms of "Indian" duplicity. Furthermore, Maya leaders often initially met Spaniards with welcoming interest, which the invaders hungrily interpreted as surrender. Imagining quick victory, Spaniards founded cities and planned colonies, only to despair over Maya rebellions, unaware that from the Maya perspective there had been neither surrender nor victory. Meanwhile, the invaders lost the advantages of surprise and unpredictability and of horses and steel; and Maya polities gained the advantages of anticipating Spanish patterns of behavior and response. As the wars stretched out, the invaders scaled back their ambitions, quietly abandoning grand visions of a colonial province stretching from Tabasco to Honduras and encompassing the whole Maya world.

In addition, somewhat paradoxically, population loss helps to explain the survival of independent Maya polities. While precise numbers remain debated (and debatable), there is no doubt that waves of epidemic disease—smallpox, typhus, measles, influenza—washed back and forth across the Maya area in the sixteenth and seventeenth centuries, to devastating effect. The gold and silver mines anticipated by the conquistador captains like the Montejos and Alvarados never materialized, leaving the Maya people themselves as the primary resource on which colonies might be built. As chronicler Gonzalo de Oviedo noted in explaining why

Acalan, settled in 1530 by Montejo as the projected new center of a peninsula-wide colony, was abandoned in 1531, "The Indians were too few to support the Spaniards, and they gave no gold in tribute but only items of food."

In many cases, population loss was the result of flight more than epidemic mortality. In all phases of the Maya–Spanish wars, from the sixteenth through nineteenth centuries, the Maya propensity to disappear infuriated non-Mayas. Some archaeologists have suggested that during the centuries of the Classic period, Maya families moved to escape oppressive regimes or instability caused by warfare or environmental change (they call this "the option of departure"). Tactical migration was thus likely a deep-rooted expression of resistance to demands by outsiders or local elites, a pattern of behavior that was exacerbated by the periodic invasion campaigns of the sixteenth century, which, in turn, helped ensure a pattern of archipelago colonization by Spaniards. Spanish settlement required sedentary Maya communities and was thus undermined when the latter became a moving target. The phenomenon intensified as the colonial period wore on, with tactical migration by Mayas in the seventeenth century causing the Spanish province of Yucatan to shrink and the kingdom of the Itza to grow.

Abandoning towns, fleeing battlefields, feigning friendship, simulating submission—these were all tactics employed with skill and to considerable effect by Maya leaders in the sixteenth century and beyond. When the Maya tactically pivoted, they preferred to do so with variations on the ambush—ideally in a confined space, whether in town or countryside, and not on open ground (where Spaniards might deploy horses or guns or use indigenous allies in numbers). Conquistadors were quick to cry foul, denouncing the "Indians" as barbarously duplicitous, offering friendships that were "false and made with evil intent" (in the words of conquistador Alonso Dávila).

What Spaniards saw as "organized treacheries and conspiracies" (as the first Merida city council put it in 1543) we can appreciate as traditional techniques of Maya resistance to invasion put to the test over and over in the sixteenth century. Such techniques proved useful in the centuries that followed, although Maya communities were forced to find new ways to meet the unprecedented challenges of incursion from the modern world.

Chapter 7
Colonizations

The study of the Maya has tended to focus on the 2,000 years of Maya history prior to the contact period (especially the thousand years surrounding the Classic period). With archaeologists and epigraphers making new discoveries almost annually, that is unlikely to change soon. But the Maya did not disappear at the close of the Classic era (no "Collapse" encompassed all Mayas) or as a result of contact with Europeans (no "Conquest" encompassed all Mayas). The Maya persisted.

That said, since the sixteenth century Maya peoples have experienced invasion and intrusion, dislocation and disruption, in every aspect of their lives and culture, on an unprecedented scale. No independent Maya states exist in the early twenty-first century. The Maya area is carved up among five nations—Mexico, Guatemala, Belize, Honduras, and El Salvador. All have treated their indigenous subjects at best with grudging acceptance and at worst with lethal brutality; Maya communities endured outbursts of genocidal violence as early as the 1520s and as recently as the 1980s. There may be roughly as many Mayas today as there were a millennium ago, but if 3 percent of the human population was then Maya, today it is less than 0.2 percent. Furthermore, as many as a quarter of today's Mayas live outside the Maya area (mostly in central Mexico and the United States), while centuries of miscegenation (with Europeans, with other indigenous

Mesoamericans, and with African-descended peoples) confound the very category of Maya.

The inclusion of non-Mayan speakers of partial Maya descent living abroad as Maya may seem to compromise the meaningfulness of the category. But migration and miscegenation, voluntary and forced, have in recent centuries been central to the history of all indigenous peoples of the Americas—all of whom have the right to claim indigenous identity in whatever sense they wish. It is up to us to respect Maya identities, be they micropatriotic, pan-Maya, or loosely diasporic, and to try to make sense of the apparent paradox of five centuries of destruction and survival, erosion and persistence.

Traditionally, the era since contact has been seen in four chronological but overlapping segments: the "Conquest period" of Spanish invasions; the Spanish colonial period of the sixteenth century to the 1820s; the period of independent republics (1820s to the present); and the modern age of tourism and globalization (since the 1970s). These segments are useful as a starting point, but their origin in colonial and national histories obscures Maya perspectives, especially the history of Maya regionalism that has characterized the Maya past for thousands of years. Maya history is not only a broad tale of victimization, with the Maya subjected to a series of colonizations, but also a continuation of the precolonial Maya story of adaptability, survival strategies, and local variations.

The struggle for autonomy

One useful way to see the Maya experience of the era of colonizations is through regional Maya struggles to retain independence or autonomy. The conquistador invasions of the sixteenth century—concentrated in what we have termed the Maya–Spanish Thirty Years War—resulted not in a blanket Spanish "Conquest of the Maya," but in an archipelago of small

Spanish colonial provinces. We deliberately use *archipelago* to describe the array of small kingdoms, city-states, and provinces in the Maya area both on the eve of the Spanish invasions and in their wake; despite the great disruption of newcomers and new diseases, that fundamental political pattern remained little altered.

Only two Spanish provinces proved to be permanent and relatively prosperous: that of "Yucatan," which comprised the peninsula's northwest, and that of "Guatemala," which comprised the southern highlands. Most *entrada* or invasion campaigns failed, and most colonies in the Maya area had by the turn of the seventeenth century been abandoned or faded to token status. For example, in the southwest, southeast, and northeast corners of Yucatan, Maya towns received occasional visits from Spanish officials or priests, with no permanent non-Maya settlers. In the east (what is now Quintana Roo and Belize), such visits eventually ceased, leaving generations of Mayas in cities like Lamanai to maintain their own, local Maya–Christian traditions.

The administrative policy of consolidating far-flung Maya villages into centralized urban spaces required the construction of new towns. In the northwestern corner of the peninsula the Franciscan order oversaw the construction of dozens of Spanish-style urban spaces, many of which were built on top of pre-Columbian ruins. The Dominican order dominated this process in the highlands. Adhering to the Laws of the Indies, first established in the Caribbean in 1512, every new town was oriented around a central plaza and a monastic complex. Maya laborers and artists constructed these impressive monuments, echoing community participation of religious construction in the pre-Columbian era. The new urban contexts became the stages for the Spanish Catholic evangelical and Hispanization campaigns, with catechism, language classes, ritual, and other forms of communal events focused in the large open-air courtyards that fronted each monastery, termed the atrium. Where successful, in the following decades, these churches became sites of civic pride for many Maya populations, and the resulting Catholicism was truly Maya as it grafted Christianity onto a substrate of indigenous belief.

Despite the inroads made by the Franciscans in Yucatan and Dominicans in Guatemala, by 1600, most of the Maya area remained outside Spanish control and in the hands of independent Maya kingdoms and polities. During the seventeenth century, the loose and fluctuating boundaries between those polities and colonial provinces shifted in favor of the Maya. The kingdom of the Itza, centered on the Peten region that had been the Classic Maya heartland, even expanded. The reversal of that trend was slow and occurred within the context of Spanish–British imperial rivalry. In the 1660s, the British established a logging settlement at the Laguna de Términos (on the gulf coast of southwest Yucatan), surviving Spanish attacks through to 1716; Maya villagers caught up in this conflict were typically enslaved by the British, thereby disappearing into the vast Atlantic slave system, or forcibly relocated into Spanish Yucatan by Spaniards or colonial Maya militias.

After 1716, British loggers refocused their activities on the other side of the peninsula's base, at the Belize River. During the eighteenth century, as they moved further upriver and onto adjacent rivers, drawing increasing Spanish attacks, Mayas fled further from the coast and independent polities disappeared or shrank. The Maya never left the Belize region completely, despite British claims that it was uninhabited, but they became few in number before a gradual recovery starting in the late nineteenth century—bolstered by Maya migration from Yucatan and Guatemala. Meanwhile, in 1697, Spanish forces overran the Itza kingdom, likewise causing an eighteenth-century Maya population drop in the Peten.

Colonial-era Maya militias were established to help defend the Spanish colonies from British and other pirate attacks, but they were also deployed against independent Maya polities, and their very existence hints at the level of autonomy that Maya communities were able to retain within the Spanish Empire. The Spanish settler minority never attempted to directly govern indigenous towns across the Americas. Instead, the settlers were administered by their own officials, termed the *república de españoles*, while native people such as the Maya governed themselves at the local level, a parallel system termed the *república de indígenas*.

The system had its limits: Maya elites were denied regional political power, at least officially and openly, and were required to act as middlemen in colonial systems of tribute collection and labor exploitation. The *encomienda* system, whereby Maya towns and villages owed unpaid (or underpaid) labor to designated Spaniards, was technically abolished in Spanish America before the Maya–Spanish wars were over, but in reality *encomiendas* persisted in the Maya colonies well into the eighteenth century. Nonetheless, local councils made up of men from the same elite lineages that had ruled in previous centuries, often with the same titles and with similar responsibilities and privileges, governed Maya municipal communities in Yucatan and Guatemala.

Maya communities in colonial provinces were not closed, in the sense that mixed-race and African-descended migrants were often welcomed—despite Spanish laws against miscegenation. For example, the movement of a very small but steady stream of Afro-Yucatecan men into Maya villages meant that rural Yucatan was in racial terms Afro-Maya by the late eighteenth century. Similar patterns took place in Guatemala, with considerable variation between the highlands and the Pacific coast. But in most regions, such men took Maya lineage or *chibal* names, spoke the language of the families into which they married, and worked as corn farmers. Maya municipal communities, the colonial-era successors of ancient polities, with their rootedness in place and lineage, were strong enough to absorb newcomers.

Prominent on the governing councils of such communities were *ah dzibob*, or "notaries," the heirs to the great writing tradition of the *aj tz'ihbob* or Classic-era artist-scribes. They wrote Mayan languages in a slightly adapted version of the Roman alphabet, helping to maintain community autonomy by recording land titles, filing lawsuits, submitting petitions, and engaging the colonial legal system in numerous ways. Petitions praising or denouncing specific Spanish officials and priests and requesting specific alleviations of tribute and labor burdens traveled from Yucatan and Guatemala to the viceroy in Mexico City and even to the king in Spain. Such petitions were penned in Mayan or in Spanish—or, in rare cases, in Nahuatl, by descendants of the Nahua warriors who had accompanied Spanish invaders during the Maya–Spanish Thirty Years War. (Figure 10 includes a depiction of Guatemalan Mayas defeated by Tlaxcalteca warriors in full battle regalia, assisted by a mounted Spanish conquistador.)

Mayanists of the early twentieth century enshrined in their textbooks the half-truth that the most prominent of the first Franciscans in Yucatan, fray Diego de Landa, burned all the surviving Maya codices and scroll books. Landa's violent 1562 campaign against "idolatry" did indeed culminate in the public burning of scores, perhaps hundreds, of books and effigies. But community elders continued to safeguard and copy many more such objects across the Maya area for the next two centuries or so. We know this because successive generations of Spanish priests described finding and destroying them—and, in very rare cases, keeping them as curiosities. Lamentably, in only a handful of cases did such mementos of priestly service in the colonies result in the permanent saving of an ancient Maya book. Don Pedro Sánchez de Aguilar, for example, a conquistador's son and a priest who conducted an anti-idolatry campaign in northeastern Yucatan in 1603–8, seems to have brought back to Spain in 1619 the invaluable, accordion-fold manuscript known to us as the Madrid Codex.

Meanwhile, Maya scribes, realizing that the traditional medium of hieroglyphs and pictographs condemned books to destruction by Spanish priests, began to transcribe the information preserved in such books into new alphabetic Mayan texts. The same notaries who recorded land sales and wills also preserved local histories and other categories of knowledge—calendrical, botanical, medicinal. Such books were partly copied from ancient hieroglyphic texts and partly drawn from Catholic dogma and other European sources. *The Books of Chilam Balam* in Yucatec and the *Popol Vuh* in K'iche' are the best known of these. The dozens of examples of *Chilam Balam* and similar manuscripts in various Mayan languages, combined with the four surviving precolonial glyphic codices and the scores of colonial-era community histories typically called *títulos*, are an invaluable cultural and intellectual heritage for present-day Mayas—and a treasure trove of source material for Mayanists.

Thus, artistic traditions, so central to Maya life before contact, were altered but not destroyed. Men continued to create and copy out books as alphabet replaced glyphs, and they continued to carve figurines to be treasured in homes—increasingly depicting saints or the Virgin Mary. Women, meanwhile, were remarkably successful in passing local weaving traditions on to successive generations; the embroidered dress or tunic (*ipil*), customarily woven on a backstrap loom, absorbed new materials and styles, yet its fundamental design and purpose—to signify the Maya wearer's identity—persists to the present.

The degree to which municipal autonomy under colonial rule was effective, despite its limitations, was cruelly exposed by the changes that hit Maya communities in the nineteenth century. Beginning in the 1820s, the governments of the new republics sought to integrate indigenous peoples more fully into the nation-state. Local political autonomy was eroded, local communal lands were broken up and their legal underpinnings destroyed, and new systems of labor exploitation were implemented. In the name of progress and modernization, such changes often deprived Maya communities of the lands they had cultivated and forests they had maintained for centuries, forcing them to work in slave-like conditions on henequen (northern Yucatan) or coffee (southern Guatemala) plantations.

By the 1840s, Maya communities had begun to resist this new conquest wave and would do so—facing increasing levels of violence in response—for the next century and a half. Conflict between ruling Hispanic factions in Yucatan, who briefly declared the peninsula an independent republic and even requested admission into the United States, slipped into civil war by 1847. Mayas fought on both sides, but when independent Maya polities of the southeast forged a temporary alliance against the government in Merida, the vast majority of Maya men at arms joined the cause. They soon took loose control of almost the entire peninsula, with Merida surrounded, before the alliance crumbled as men returned home to plant their cornfields. Reclassified by the Hispanic elite as a race war called the "War of the Castes," the conflict flared up again in 1850, simmering away in the east for the rest of the century, with the capital city of the independent Mayas not taken by Mexican government troops until 1901.

Sustained by the political–religious cult of the Talking Cross, an oracular icon that prophesized for the indigenous population, the independent Mayas were called *cruzob* (the Spanish word for "cross" in the Yucatec Maya plural). Formally founded in 1849, the *cruzob* state was recognized as an independent nation by the British Empire, whose colony of British Honduras (now Belize) bordered the *cruzob* to the south, until 1893 (when Britons were killed in a *cruzob* seizure of the Hispanic Yucatecan outpost of Bacalar).

Although after 1901 the *cruzob* polity was a shadow of its former self, *cruzob* general Francisco May did not sign a formal peace treaty with the Mexican government until 1935, while Mayas maintained Talking Crosses in southeastern Maya villages and ancient sites (such as Tulum) into the late twentieth century. It was not the Mexican government, but the onset of international tourism beginning in the 1970s that finally destroyed the vestiges of Maya autonomy in southeastern Yucatan; over 350,000 tourists now visit Tulum every year, in some months drawing more international visitors than any other archaeological site in Mexico and Guatemala.

To the south, meanwhile, there were sporadic Maya uprisings in the eighteenth century in reaction to perceived Spanish violations of the moral economy of the colonial regime. That is, the Maya accepted Spanish colonialism in return for limited levels of exploitation. When Maya leaders believed those limits had been exceeded, they organized revolts; one took place in Chiapas in 1712, and three others erupted in highland Guatemala between 1735 and 1768. With the colonial regime gone after 1821, that moral economy was again subject to top-down abuses and Maya attempts at remediation and renegotiation. In contrast to mid-nineteenth-century Yucatan, Mayas in Guatemala received relative respite under the regime of Rafael Carrera; of partial Maya descent, he used Maya rebels to lead an uprising in 1838, going on to rule Guatemala and dominate Central American politics until his death in 1865. Still, even Carrera, toward the end of his rule, encouraged the spread of coffee farms and therefore encroachment on Maya lands and exploitation of Maya workers.

After Carrera, the Hispanic elite moved quickly to sweep away what remained of legal protections on Maya lands and all traces of indigenous community autonomy. For the next eighty years, a series of authoritarian presidents and military dictators turned Guatemala into a land where a wealthy elite minority owned most of the land, devoting it to export monoculture (most notably of coffee), and an impoverished majority (mostly Mayas) toiled under abysmal conditions without political freedoms.

The pendulum began to swing back in 1944. With fascism on the run worldwide, Guatemalans were able to expel the army from political office and elect civil presidents whose platforms promised reforms that would return Maya communities' access to traditional lands, political rights, and at least some semblance of autonomy. But the reformers' paternalistic vision of the nation compromised respect for Maya autonomy. Furthermore, "the Guatemalan Spring," as it was dubbed, lasted only a decade.

In 1954, a military coup, organized by the CIA and backed by the US government, put the military back in power. A series of repressive regimes were sustained by the increased use of state terror campaigns, aided by US financial and military support, inspiring organized Maya community protest and the formation of non-Maya guerilla organizations. This undeclared civil war cost almost 10,000 lives in the 1960s and more than that in the 1970s. Maya villagers were caught in the crossfire more and more, accused by the military government of providing support for guerillas. In 1978, the army's massacre of over 100 unarmed Q'eqchi' Mayas, including children, marked the escalation of the civil war into a genocidal campaign against the Maya. Entire Maya villages were wiped out. By the early 1990s, when the conflict moved toward a United Nations–sponsored peace agreement, some 200,000 people had been killed, many after being "disappeared" or tortured, almost all of them Mayas. A million people had been displaced, a tenth of them into countries to the north—again, the vast majority of them Mayas.

The war thus exacerbated the negative impact on Maya communities of large-scale export agriculture; just as anti-indigenous violence had combined with economic liberalism in the nineteenth century to displace Mayas from their homes and lands, so did neoliberal economic policies combine with state-sponsored violence in the twentieth century to foment genocidal outbursts and create a diaspora of Maya migrants and refugees.

As the civil war wound down in Guatemala, Maya communities sought new ways to recover, regroup, and renew the struggle for some autonomy within the larger context of powerful nation-states and increasing globalization. The quincentennial in 1992 of Columbus's first voyage spurred Maya intellectuals and activists to present their view of the past five centuries. The resulting Maya intellectual renaissance helped forge a pan-Maya movement that has been slowly spreading from Guatemala to other Maya regions. Also in 1992, Rigoberta Menchú won the Nobel Peace Prize. A K'iche' Maya whose family were tortured and killed in Guatemala in the early 1980s, Menchú's 1984 memoir (despite subsequent controversy over how much of it was her personal story and how much an amalgamation of Maya experiences), her Nobel award, and her subsequent decades of activism all helped to give the cause of Maya autonomy an international profile.

At the same time, worsening economic conditions in Chiapas, combined with political corruption and the impact of refugees from the war in neighboring Guatemala, provoked the 1994 uprising of Tsotsil and Tseltal Mayas in that Mexican state. The government dispatched the army, but the feared violent repression of the Zapatista National Liberation Army and massacre of Maya villagers did not occur. With the dawn of the Internet age, the Zapatistas were able to use the global news media and social media to garner sympathy and support. Their army evolved into a political party and their rebellion into a movement, and their campaign became one of many across the Maya area to use political, legislative, and legal means to regain or procure some autonomy for indigenous communities. In southern Belize, for example, the Q'eqchi' Maya have been fighting incursions on their lands and their community autonomy, engaging the government at a national and—as in the Chiapas and Guatemalan Maya cases—an international level.

Lost and found

Meanwhile, parallel to the Maya experience of colonialism and nationalism from the sixteenth to twentieth centuries, the story of the ancient Maya continued to unfold. The first generations of Spaniards who saw Maya towns and cities tended not to question the simple fact that local people had constructed them and continued to live in or near them. Diego de Landa, for example, remarked that it was obvious that monumental structures in the peninsula "have not been built by any people other than these Indians." But that perception shifted among Spaniards—and by extension Europeans and then white North Americans—over the subsequent centuries. As a result, it became possible for ruined Maya cities to be "discovered" (again and again) and the enigma of who built them to be forged.

That shift in perception took place for several reasons. First, long-term patterns of migration in the Maya area—especially the changes that underpinned the so-called Collapse in the central region—meant that some towns and cities were already abandoned by the time Spaniards invaded and explored the area. Second, the impact of Conquest-era violence and epidemic disease caused dramatic population decline across all Maya regions, even those not incorporated into Spanish colonial provinces. A century after the first major Spanish invasions into Maya kingdoms in the 1520s, the total Maya population had fallen by some 80 percent (from very approximately 10 to 2 million).

Third, in the regions where colonies were established, Spaniards imposed policies of *congregación*, or forced resettlement, in which the surviving residents of scattered towns were made to move into a central town—to facilitate the Maya conversion to Christianity and their exploitation as a source of labor and local products. At the same time, some cities were given an architectural facelift or reconstruction. In Yucatan, for example, as Tiho became Merida and Itzmal became Izamal, European-styled buildings replaced palaces and other Maya houses, temples were razed, and friars ordered churches to be built on top of pyramid bases. Such architectural transformations further eclipsed in the European mind the notion that "the Indians" around them were related to those who had built great cities in those same locations.

The change in perception was gradual. Early Spanish visitors to ancient sites in the Maya area described what they saw on the assumption that the builders had been local. The Franciscan Jacinto Garrido, for example, explored Palenque in the 1530s and described it in detail, and Diego García de Palacio vividly depicted Copan in a 1576 letter to the Spanish king. Neither imagined foreign architects or external influences. Similarly, over a century later, on the eve of the 1697 Spanish destruction of the Itza Maya kingdom in the Peten, missionary priests traveling between that kingdom and the colony in Yucatan came across Tikal and Yaxchilan, later relating what they saw without questioning that it had been built by the Maya—even if they did not label it as such.

Yet even in these early descriptions one finds the seeds of the sense of mystery that later explorers and writers would nurture. Garrido was fascinated by the hieroglyphic texts he found at Palenque, but imagined they were "Chaldean letters" (that Aramaic language, written in a version of Syriac script, was probably the only nonalphabetic example he knew). García de Palacio, struck by the "superb" and "skillful" nature of Copan's ancient buildings, concluded that "they could never have been built by a people as primitive as the natives of this province." Here, at least he attributed the ruins to people we classify as Maya, giving credence to local lore that "in ancient times there came from Yucatan a great lord, who built these edifices" (an intriguing echo, perhaps, of the Teotihuacano founding of the dynasty that ruled Copan from 426 to 820).

By the eighteenth century, however, it was widely assumed that the ancient stone structures of ruined Maya cities could not have been the work of the ancestors of the local people who lived near or even among such buildings. In the second half of the century, Spanish settlers, priests, and officials regularly visited, damaged, and looted Palenque, for example. One visitor, Antonio del Río, expressed what had become prevailing opinion when he conjectured that while the ancient Romans may not have actually conquered the Maya, Romans must have visited their lands, inspiring "the natives to embrace during their visit an idea of the arts as a reward for their hospitality."

In the nineteenth century, explorer-writers who published accounts and visual representations of Maya ruins repeated del Río's sentiment and were overwhelmingly convinced that they were discovering (over and over) a civilization with Old World origins. Influential gentlemen-scholars such as Jean-Frédéric de Waldeck and Lord Kingsborough, for example, looked for evidence of ancient Roman, Greek, Egyptian, Hebrew, or Hindu influence. Not finding it, they imagined or invented it. When these Europeans went to draw the art and architecture of the ancient Maya cities, they stylistically altered monuments to appear more like Near Eastern material artifacts. They included elephants and other animals not indigenous to the Americas, but ubiquitous in other forms of "exotic" art. These early prephotographic depictions thus reflected the tropes of the era—mostly notably Romanticism and a glorification of European imperialism; they invented visual evidence for the theory that Europeans of previous millennia, not the ancient Maya, created Maya civilization.

Inspired by Waldeck, the American traveler-writer and diplomat John Lloyd Stephens also "discovered" sites such as Palenque and Uxmal, taking with him an English architect, Frederick Catherwood. Stephens's vivid descriptions, illustrated by Catherwood's evocative lithographs, have sold well ever since, helping to perpetuate interest in the Maya from the 1840s to the present. Although Stephens gave more credit to local "Indians" than Waldeck and others did, he nonetheless perpetuated the idea that Maya history was a riddle to be solved.

After Stephens and Catherwood, the flow of interest in the Maya—we can now start to call it Maya studies—followed two great streams. The devotees in one continued to imagine external origins for the art and achievements found in Maya ruins, and the stream has remained overwhelmingly amateur (or at least nonacademic), highly speculative, and oriented toward outlandish explanations. One Mayanist dubbed it "the lunatic fringe of Maya archaeology." Just as Waldeck had seen elephants in Maya art, so were late-nineteenth-century explorer-archaeologists such as Désiré Charnay and Augustus Le Plongeon—the lasting value of their photographs aside—convinced that Maya civilization was inextricably and mysteriously linked to ancient Asia or the Mediterranean. Le Plongeon, for example, insisted on Maya–Egypt connections via the lost continent of Atlantis; he influenced the English pseudoscientist-writer James Churchward, who argued in the early twentieth century that the ancient Maya (like the ancient Egyptians) were remnants of the civilization of a lost Pacific continent called Mu.

The antiquarian and public fascination with ancient Egypt, which had contributed to the flow of the nonacademic, pseudoscientific stream of Maya studies in the early twentieth century, gave way in the 1960s to the newly popular "ancient aliens" theory—whereby early human beings learned civilization from extraterrestrials at the time of "paleocontact." The most prominent purveyor of this theory has been the Swiss author Erich von Däniken, whose books on paleocontact have sold close to 100 million copies. In *Chariots of the Gods?*, first published in 1968 and by some reckonings one of the three best-selling books of all time, the carved lid of the sarcophagus of K'inich Janaab Pakal I, the *k'uhul ajaw* of seventh-century Palenque, depicts Pakal as a spaceman sitting at the controls of a rocket ship.

As absurdly fanciful as such ideas may seem and as much as professional Maya scholars are able to dismantle utterly all "lunatic fringe" theories of cultural diffusionism, lost continents, and paleocontact with aliens, they remain hugely popular. They reach more readers and television viewers than do the well-evidenced scientific reports of professional archaeologists. Wrong-headed notions regarding Maya mysteries mislead the public and perpetuate a neocolonial assumption that nonwhite peoples are incapable of achieving anything as impressive as Maya civilization.

The other stream of Maya studies that followed Stephens and Catherwood was built from the start on the premise that ancient Maya civilization was autochthonous—that it was part of the larger civilization of Mesoamerica (stretching from northern Mexico to the southern edges of the Maya area) and influenced by contact only with other Mesoamerican cultures. Indeed, this stream, which led to the development of professional, university-based, academic fields of Maya studies—primarily but not exclusively that of archaeology—came to define those two interrelated civilizations (Mesoamerica and the Maya) in the twentieth century.

During the genesis of scientific archaeology in 1880–1920, scholars such as Alfred Maudslay transformed the field of Maya studies into a systematic effort to document, describe, draw, and photograph every Maya glyph, monument, and structure. In the decades that followed, multidisciplinary team projects made modern Mayanist archaeology possible. Yet, despite the emphasis on data collection over mere speculation and the reliance of peer evaluation over individual theorizing, the academic stream of the twentieth century did not completely escape its common origins with the nonacademic stream. Professional gentlemen-scholars were in some ways the heirs of the amateur gentlemen-explorers.

As a result, the ancient Maya became romanticized as peace-loving farmers ruled by stargazing theocrats, the very exemplars of a civilized people. As most of the glyphs deciphered before the 1970s related to astronomy and calendrics, an impression was created that these topics were the only human experiences of interest to the ancient Maya elites. It is thus hardly surprising that the general public was so receptive to the idea that extraterrestrials taught civilization to the Classic Maya. Because of this academic investment in the "peace-loving" Maya, for much of the twentieth century, the Maya were almost "non-human," as archaeologist George Stuart put it, "gentle astronomers forever gazing towards the sky, and never doing anything that other people did." And because most of the fieldwork prior to the 1970s focused on the monumental structures in the city centers, the acropolis of palaces and temples, those centers were seen as ceremonial only and the cities not really as cities at all. The true farmers of the ancient Maya world had yet to be located archaeologically.

The most prominent proponent of this view, Sir Eric Thompson, exercised a controlling influence over Maya studies until his death in 1975, after which previously marginalized counteropinions were given fresh air. As breakthroughs in hieroglyphic decipherment gathered pace toward the end of the century and archaeological work increasingly turned to smaller sites, the suburbs, and the living spaces of the nonelite, the Maya emerged as more urban, more warlike—more like other human civilizations.

This is not to say that the element of mystery—so central to the other, nonacademic stream of Maya studies—has faded from serious Maya scholarship. Mayanists sometimes still fall under the spell of the interpretations we package for the public and in pursuit of funding for costly archaeological projects. As a result, we sometimes overdramatize two dimensions of our work—discovery and disappearance. Just as Spanish priests and European gentleman-explorers discovered sites over and over in past centuries, so do Mayanists routinely "discover" long-known palaces and cities.

A misleading paradox thus persists: the Maya remain a symbol of civilizational collapse and population disappearance, yet scholars and activists continue to stress that the Maya vanished neither at the end of the Classic period nor under the onslaught of colonialism and nationalism. Maya civilization still awaits its discoverers, yet it has never ceased to exist and be visible.

The challenge of adaptation

Within the varied history of Maya struggles to retain some degree of political autonomy, Maya communities and individuals also confronted a seemingly endless series of introductions and innovations—from imported material goods, to new diseases and diets, to cultural and technological changes. Since the sixteenth century, adopting and adapting to new objects, domesticated animals, foods, religious ideas, and concepts of family and community has often been a double-edged sword.

There was no upside to the viruses and other pathogens that Old World peoples and animals introduced to the Maya, whose population was hit repeatedly in the sixteenth and seventeenth centuries, falling to some 10 to 20 percent of its precolonial level before slowly recovering from the eighteenth century on. But the introduction of Old World domesticated animals—most notably horses, cattle, sheep, pigs, and chickens—contributed to a more diverse diet and the further development of cuisines. Because Mayas were not tempted by (or did not have the opportunity for) many Spanish habits, such as excessive consumption of meat and wheat and the daily use of oils and animal fats, the impact on Maya health was, on balance, positive. On the other hand, the environmental impact of cattle and sheep was not positive, nor was the encroachment on Maya lands of cattle ranches owned by non-Mayas—especially in the eighteenth and nineteenth centuries.

Likewise, while Mayas readily embraced many new crops, such as new varieties of citrus trees, the suitability of some regions of the Maya area to sugar and coffee farming had a devastating impact on local communities (most notably in late nineteenth- and early twentieth-century Guatemala). Sugar also brought cheap cane alcohol (*aguardiente*), more damaging to the health than the traditional fermented beverages, whose consumption had often been restricted by its accompanying social and religious rituals— such as Guatemalan *chicha* (from maize) and Yucatecan *balche'* (from tree bark and honey). Introduced crops for which there is external demand continue to represent both opportunity and danger for Maya farmers; for example, Kaqchikel Maya farmers at the turn of the twenty-first century were torn between growing maize and beans for local consumption or broccoli for profitable but fickle export markets.

The story is similar with the history of introduced material goods and technologies over the past five centuries. Iron and steel made farming easier; gunpowder made fishing and hunting easier. But the ability to clear more forest and reduce its wildlife was a mixed blessing. Later, the transportation and communication revolutions—from railroads to buses, cars, and motorcycles; from telephones and television to the Internet—infiltrated and influenced Maya communities, making possible a positive Maya diaspora. That diaspora comprised not only war refugees, but also untraumatized families seeking distant work opportunities (whether in the United States, Mexico City, or Cancun and the ever-expanding Maya Riviera) while maintaining community connections.

The history of Mayan languages since the sixteenth century is likewise one of gain and loss, change and persistence. On the one hand, the number of Mayan languages declined, while surviving tongues lost vocabulary and grammatical features under the influence of Spanish and English. The educational systems of modern states were run—until this century—in Spanish, with the reading or speaking of Mayan typically banned. Most Mayan speakers are bilingual (or multilingual), and that number continues to increase.

On the other hand, Mayan languages also gained vocabulary through contact with Spanish and English—just as they did through contact with Nahuatl before and during the sixteenth century, a reminder of the fact that change is intrinsic to language. Furthermore, indigenous language revitalization has been aided by modern phenomena—television, the Internet, globalization— that initially seemed to undermine Mayan languages. Mayan can now increasingly be heard online in various contexts, from formal language lessons to videos of musicians singing and rapping in Yucatec.

Change, adoption, and hybridization are cultural constants— whether the focus is on ideas and practices, living things, or material objects. This is true for all societies, not just those of the Maya; and it has been true for all Maya history, not just the colonial and modern era. The result has been gain as well as loss, cultural enrichment, and civilizational development, not just invasion and victimization. Throughout the Maya world of the early twenty-first century—from the pan-Mayanists of Guatemala and the Zapatistas of Chiapas, to indigenous community leaders and local politicians in Yucatan and Belize, to diasporic Maya intellectuals, activists, and wage laborers—cultural fusion fortifies the struggle for autonomy.

Mayas have refused to give up what makes them *them*. At the same time, they have rejected a simple or superficial promotion of traditional cultural traits, choosing to keep discussions of identity open and borrowing freely from diverse ideological, cultural, and political forms. As a result, Mayas are constantly creating dynamic new hybrid forms and definitions of what *Maya* means. That fact applies most obviously to the twenty-first century, but equally to centuries past: to the way in which the Maya adopted and adapted the Roman alphabet, for example, or the myriad ways in which Maya communities embraced and localized Catholicism to forge distinct regional Maya Christianities. Regardless of whether such Christianities were maintained by Franciscan friars and elders of the Pech dynasty in northwest Yucatan in the late sixteenth century, by independent Maya priests in Belizean cities in the seventeenth century, or by Protestant pastors and community leaders in Guatemala in the early twenty-first century, they are all Maya religious forms as much as was the religion of Classic-era Tikal. Indeed, the challenge of adaptation, like the struggle for autonomy, is not new to the Maya, nor was it new to them in the sixteenth century.

A twenty-first-century Maya world

The Maya experience of the centuries since contact has fomented a kind of cultural hybridity; Maya civilization has continued to evolve in contact with the outside world, as well as according to its own internal dynamics and traditions. The result is that some cultural aspects of Maya life today seem "old-fashioned" or transparently descended from past practices and beliefs. Others seem decidedly modern or imported, most obviously with Maya peoples connected to the outside world via new technologies or patterns of personal mobility. Regardless of the scholarly take on this modern culture, it is important to recognize that the Maya themselves would not conceptualize their society as "mixed" or "hybridized" in the least; it is a self-sustained cultural system, wholly independent of the historical cultures that produced it.

The Maya world in the early twenty-first century is highly diffuse and varied, not only stretched across the national borders between Mexico and Guatemala, Belize and Honduras, but also extending into the United States, Canada, and Europe. Some Mayas lead highly localized lives and others are highly mobile and migrant. There are rural Maya communities and urban ones, Mayan-speaking communities and those that are bilingual or only Spanish speaking. Maya religion today includes an increasingly broad array of beliefs and practices drawn variously from Catholicism, Protestantism, and traditional folk devotion. Yet despite this multiplicity of cultural arrangements, we can still arguably speak meaningfully of a Maya world—of Maya civilization—in the twenty-first century.

Acknowledgments

We are grateful to Traci Ardren, Scott Doebler, Mary Kate Kelly, Maxime Lamoureux St-Hilaire, Edward Fischer, and Katherine Godfrey for comments and corrections made on earlier drafts; and to Norman Hammond and an anonymous external reader for their extensive and expert thoughts. We also thank VSI editor extraordinaire Nancy Toff, for her encouragement, patience, and skillful editing. Thanks too are due to our Penn State department heads and college deans for their support, and to the Penn State students in History 302 (Fall 2019) for their feedback.

We would also like to acknowledge the Mayanists who have supported and nurtured us with their friendship, collegiality, or mentorship over the decades, and thereby made myriad contributions to this book; they include, in addition to those mentioned above, Gerardo Aldana, Victoria Bricker, Marcello Canuto, Mark Christensen, John Chuchiak, Wolfgang Gabbert, Elizabeth Graham, Ruth Gubler, Sarah Jackson, Rosemary Joyce, Jeff Kowalski, William Hanks, Stephen Houston, Susan Kepecs, Richard Leventhal, Victoria Lyall, Patricia McAnany, Mary Miller, Sergio Quezada, Terry Rugeley, Andrew Scherer, Mark Van Stone, Paul Sullivan, Jorge Victoria Ojeda, David Webster, Lorraine Williams-Beck, Jason Yaeger, and Marc Zender.

References

In addition to numerous more specialized books and articles, we
found the following six books to be especially useful: Norman
Hammond, *The Maya* (London: Folio Society, 2000; also available
in earlier editions and from other publishers as *Ancient Maya
Civilization*); David Webster, *The Fall of the Ancient Maya:
Solving the Mystery of the Maya Collapse* (London: Thames &
Hudson, 2002); Arthur Demarest, *Ancient Maya: The Rise and
Fall of a Rainforest Civilization* (Cambridge: Cambridge
University Press, 2004); Stephen Houston and Takeshi Inomata,
The Classic Maya (Cambridge: Cambridge University Press,
2009); Mary Ellen Miller and Megan E. O'Neil, *Maya Art and
Architecture* (New York: Thames & Hudson, 2012); and
Michael D. Coe and Stephen Houston, *The Maya*, 9th ed. (New
York: Thames & Hudson, 2015; originally published by Coe in
1966; because Maya studies have evolved so dramatically, we do
not recommend earlier editions).

The "deeper realities" quote in Chapter 1 is from Houston and Inomata,
The Classic Maya, xiii. Our discussion in Chapter 2 of the Palenque
sweat bath texts draws on Stephen D. Houston, "Symbolic
Sweatbaths of the Maya: Architectural Meaning in the Cross Group
at Palenque, Mexico," *Latin American Antiquity* 7, no. 2 (1996):
132–51; that of El Mirador draws on various publications by
Richard Hansen; and that of the Yaxchilan–Piedras Negras rivalry
draws on conversations with, and conference presentations by,
Andrew Scherer (who is a principal researcher in the region, along
with Charles Golden, building on earlier work by Houston and
others); also see Zach Zorich, "Defending a Jungle Kingdom,"
Archaeology (September/October 2011): 34–38 (Scherer quote, 38).

In Chapter 4, we paraphrase Stephen D. Houston, Oswaldo Chinchilla Mazariegos, and David Stuart, *The Decipherment of Ancient Maya Writing* (Norman: University of Oklahoma Press, 2001) ("ever devised," 3), as well as several passages in Miller and O'Neil, *Maya Art and Architecture*. For Chapter 5, we relied again on the work of Houston, including *The Gifted Passage: Young Men in Classic Maya Art and Text* (New Haven, CT: Yale University Press, 2018); on Scott R. Hutson, *The Ancient Urban Maya: Neighborhoods, Inequality, and Built Form* (Gainesville: University Press of Florida, 2016); and on Demarest, *Ancient Maya*, especially Chapter 6 (e.g., "true secret" quote, 120).

For coverage of the sixteenth to nineteenth centuries in Chapters 6–7, we relied on the relevant Further Reading items listed below and on our own work; specifically, in addition to items listed below, Matthew Restall's *The Maya World: Yucatec Culture and Society, 1550–1850* (Stanford, CA: Stanford University Press, 1997); *The Black Middle: Africans, Mayas, and Spaniards in Colonial Yucatan* (Stanford, CA: Stanford University Press, 2009); and, with Mark Z. Christensen, *Return to Ixil: Maya Society in an Eighteenth-Century Yucatec Town* (Boulder: University Press of Colorado, 2019); as well as Amara Solari's *Maya Ideologies of the Sacred: The Transfiguration of Space in Colonial Yucatan* (Austin: University of Texas Press, 2013) and *Idolizing Mary: Maya-Catholic Icons in Yucatan, Mexico* (University Park: Pennsylvania State University Press, 2019).

Sources in Chapter 7 include Demarest, *Ancient Maya*, especially Chapter 3 ("lunatic fringe" is his phrase, 34); Webster, *The Fall*; Lovell, *A Beauty That Hurts*; Garrett Fagan, ed. *Archaeological Fantasies: How Pseudoarchaeology Misrepresents the Past and Misleads the Public* (Abingdon-on-Thames, UK: Routledge, 2006); and Matthew Restall and Amara Solari, *2012 and the End of the World: The Western Roots of the Maya Apocalypse* (Lanham, MD: Rowman & Littlefield, 2011). The US historian quoted in Chapter 6 ("stubborn," etc.) is Robert Chamberlain. The "option of departure" archaeologists are Houston and Inomata. "Maya intellectual renaissance" was a phrase coined and defined by Victor Montejo (in various publications). Our "hybrid forms" passage paraphrases Edward F. Fischer and Peter Benson, *Broccoli & Desire: Global Connections and Maya Struggles in Postwar Guatemala* (Stanford, CA: Stanford University Press, 2006), 153–54 (and Fischer's larger body of work was also useful).

Further reading

By way of overviews of the ancient Maya, we recommend the six books listed under "References," specifically, those by Coe and Houston, by Demarest, and by Hammond for general overviews, those by Webster and by Houston and Inomata for the Classic period, and that by Miller and O'Neil on art. There are many others, however, some as well written, up to date, and useful as those we relied on. There are also many relevant encyclopedias. We recommend:

Carrasco, Davíd. *The Oxford Encyclopedia of Mesoamerican Cultures*. Oxford: Oxford University Press, 2001.

Evans, Susan Toby, and David Webster, eds. *Archaeology of Ancient Mexico and Central America*. New York: Garland, 2001.

Witschey, Walter R. T. *Encyclopedia of the Ancient Maya*. Lanham, MD: Rowman & Littlefield, 2016.

The best overviews of Maya hieroglyphic writing and the history of its decipherment are:

Coe, Michael D. *Breaking the Maya Code*. Rev. ed. London: Thames & Hudson, 1999.

Houston, Stephen D., Oswaldo Chinchilla Mazariegos, and David Stuart. *The Decipherment of Ancient Maya Writing*. Norman: University of Oklahoma Press, 2001.

An engaging introduction to both Maya writing and art is:

Stone, Andrea, and Marc Zender, *Reading Maya Art: A Hieroglyphic Guide to Ancient Maya Painting and Sculpture* (London: Thames & Hudson, 2011).

The literature on Maya art is incredibly vast, but here is a selection of respected sources:

Doyle, James. *Architecture and the Origins of Preclassic Maya Politics*. Cambridge: Cambridge University Press, 2017.

Halpern, Christina T. *Maya Figurines: Intersections between State and Household*. Austin: University of Texas Press, 2014.

Houston, Stephen. *The Life Within: Classic Maya and the Matter of Permanence*. New Haven, CT: Yale University Press, 2014.

Miller, Mary, and Claudia Brittenham. *The Spectacle of the Late Maya Court: Reflections on the Murals of Bonampak*. Austin: University of Texas Press, 2013.

To elucidate gender in the ancient Maya World, we recommend:

Joyce, Rosemary A. *Gender and Power in Prehispanic Mesoamerica*. Austin: University of Texas Press, 2000.

For more on the Toltec–Maya relationship discussed in Chapter 6, we recommend:

Kowalski, Jeff Karl, and Cynthia Kristan-Graham, eds. *Twin Tollans: Chichén Itzá, Tula, and the Epiclassic to Early Postclassic Mesoamerican World*. Washington, DC: Dumbarton Oaks Research Library and Collection, 2011.

On Maya monarchies, see:

Martin, Simon, and Nikolai Grube. Rev. ed. *Chronicles of the Maya Kings and Queens*. London: Thames & Hudson, 2008.

On cities, see:

Hutson, Scott R. *The Ancient Urban Maya: Neighborhoods, Inequality, and Built Form*. Gainesville: University Press of Florida, 2016.

On looting, see:

Tremain, Cara G., and Donna Yates, eds. *The Market for Mesoamerica: Reflections on the Sale of Pre-Columbian Antiquities*. Gainesville: University Press of Florida, 2019.

For further reading on the periods of the Spanish invasions of conquest, of colonialism, and of modern nation-states, we recommend the following:

Clendinnen, Inga. *Ambivalent Conquests: Maya and Spaniard in Yucatan, 1517–1570*. 1987. 2nd ed., Cambridge: Cambridge University Press, 2003.

Grandin, Greg. *The Blood of Guatemala: A History of Race and Nation*. Durham, NC: Duke University Press, 2000.

Jones, Grant D. *The Conquest of the Last Maya Kingdom*. Stanford, CA: Stanford University Press, 1998.

Lovell, W. George. *A Beauty That Hurts: Life and Death in Guatemala*. 4th ed. Toronto: Between the Lines, 2019.

Lovell, W. George, Christopher Lutz, and Wendy Kramer. *Strike Fear in the Land: Pedro de Alvarado and the Conquest of Guatemala, 1524–1541*. Norman: University of Oklahoma Press, 2020.

Patch, Robert W. *Maya Revolt and Revolution in the Eighteenth Century*. Armonk, NY: M. E. Sharpe, 2002.

Restall, Matthew. *Maya Conquistador*. Boston: Beacon Press, 1998.

Restall, Matthew, and Florine Asselbergs. *Invading Guatemala: Spanish, Nahua, and Maya Accounts of the Conquest Wars*. University Park: Pennsylvania State University Press, 2008.

Sullivan, Paul. *Xuxub Must Die: The Lost Histories of a Murder on the Yucatan*. Pittsburgh, PA: University of Pittsburgh Press, 2004.

The scholarly literature on Maya history since contact is even vaster than that on the ancient Maya. But whereas the latter are, almost by definition, only about the Maya, studies of the colonial and modern periods are often not exclusively focused on the Maya experience.

Index